LOVE NOTES
for couples

90 Days of Love Language
Minute Devotions

GARY CHAPMAN

TYNDALE
MOMENTUM®

The Tyndale nonfiction imprint

Visit Tyndale online at tyndale.com.

Visit Tyndale Momentum online at tyndalemomentum.com.

TYNDALE, Tyndale Momentum, The One Year, One Year, LeatherLike, and Tyndale's quill logo are registered trademarks of Tyndale House Publishers. The Tyndale Momentum logo and the One Year logo are trademarks of Tyndale House Publishers. Tyndale Momentum is the nonfiction imprint of Tyndale House Publishers, Carol Stream, Illinois.

The 5 Love Languages® and The Five Love Languages® are registered trademarks of The Moody Bible Institute of Chicago. Love Language™ and Love Language Minute™ are common law trademarks of The Moody Bible Institute of Chicago. *The 5 Love Languages®* is a book published by Northfield Publishing, an imprint of Moody Publishers. *Love Language Minute™* is a short radio series of programs aired by The Moody Bible Institute of Chicago, from which *The One Year Love Language Minute Devotional* and *Love Notes for Couples* have been adapted. The radio program series recordings are copyrighted by The Moody Bible Institute of Chicago. All rights reserved. Used with permission. For reprint or other use rights, contact Moody Publishers at moodypublishers.com.

Love Notes for Couples: 90 Days of Love Language Minute Devotions

Copyright © 2020 by Gary D. Chapman. All rights reserved.

Devotional content adapted from *The One Year Love Language Minute Devotional* published by Tyndale House Publishers under ISBN 978-1-4143-2973-4 in 2009.

Designed by Libby Dykstra

Cover photograph of couple copyright © courtneyk/Getty Images. All rights reserved.

Cover photograph of clouds by Eberhard Grossgasteiger on Unsplash.

Back cover photograph of surfboard by Joschko Hammermann on Unsplash

Unless otherwise indicated, all Scripture quotations are taken from the *Holy Bible*, New Living Translation, copyright © 1996, 2004, 2015 by Tyndale House Foundation. (Some quotations may be from the 2007 edition of the NLT.) Used by permission of Tyndale House Publishers, Carol Stream, Illinois 60188. All rights reserved.

Scripture quotations marked ESV are taken from the ESV® Bible (The Holy Bible, English Standard Version®), copyright © 2001 by Crossway, a publishing ministry of Good News Publishers. Used by permission. All rights reserved.

Scripture quotations marked KJV are taken from the *Holy Bible*, King James Version.

Scripture quotations marked NASB are taken from the New American Standard Bible,® copyright © 1960, 1962, 1963, 1968, 1971, 1972, 1973, 1975, 1977, 1995 by The Lockman Foundation. Used by permission.

Scripture quotations marked NIV are taken from the Holy Bible, *New International Version,® NIV.®* Copyright © 1973, 1978, 1984, 2011 by Biblica, Inc.® Used by permission. All rights reserved worldwide.

Scripture quotations marked NKJV are taken from the New King James Version,® copyright © 1982 by Thomas Nelson, Inc. Used by permission. All rights reserved.

For information about special discounts for bulk purchases, please contact Tyndale House Publishers at csresponse@tyndale.com, or call 1-800-323-9400.

ISBN 978-1-4964-4663-3

Printed in the United States of America.

26	25	24	23	22	21	20
7	6	5	4	3	2	1

Introduction

When two people commit to each other—and especially when they commit to communicating their love to each other through the five love languages—positive change occurs. Time and time again, I've seen the power of God transform relationships.

The building blocks of marriage—such as good communication, respect, unconditional love, and forgiveness—are foundational to any romantic relationship. And learning to identify and speak your spouse's love language will benefit you and your loved one at any stage. I tend to use the language of marriage when I write, because my background is in marriage counseling, but if you're dating or engaged, you will find plenty of helpful information here as well.

You can use this devotional individually or sit down together as a couple to read it each day. Use the prayer at the end of each devotion as a starting point for your own prayer—whether you pray silently together or aloud, one at a time. In just a few minutes, you can discover encouraging biblical insights.

As an added feature, this devotional includes the

Love Note Starter Kit, which you will find in the back of the book. This "kit" includes a few simple prompts to help you compose a love note to your spouse that will directly address your respective love languages.

Whether your relationship is strong or struggling, stable or challenging, my prayer is that this devotional will encourage you and give you renewed joy in each other. May your relationship be strengthened as you focus on loving and growing together.

Gary Chapman

"I Really Appreciate That"

Whoever wants to be first among you must be the
slave of everyone else. For even the Son of Man
came not to be served but to serve others and
to give his life as a ransom for many.

MARK 10:44-45

The theme of the Christian life is serving Christ by
serving others. Jesus came to earth to serve others—
first by his love, his teaching, and his healings, and
ultimately by his death. When we serve others, we are
not only serving Christ, but we are being Christlike. So
why not begin developing an attitude of service in our
closest relationship? The fact is, we do acts of service
for each other every day. However, we don't often talk
about them, and consequently, we begin to take them
for granted.

I want to suggest a little communication exercise
that will bring service to the front burner. It's a game
called I Really Appreciate That. Here's how you play it:
The husband might say to the wife, "One way I served
you today was by putting away a load of laundry." The

wife might respond, "I really appreciate that." Then she says, "One way I served you today was by cooking dinner." The husband responds, "I really appreciate that." Play the game once a day for a week, and you will become more aware of the acts of service that you are already doing for each other. You will elevate them to a place of importance by talking about them. If you have children, let them hear you playing the game, and they'll want to get in on the fun.

Lord Jesus, thank you for your example of service.
Please transform me more each day into your image.
Help us as a couple to serve each other with love
and to show our appreciation for each other.

Looking at the Positive

Some people make cutting remarks,
but the words of the wise bring healing.
PROVERBS 12:18

One of the most powerful things we can do to enhance the seasons of our marriage is to choose a winning attitude. How do we do this?

First, we must admit our negative thinking. As long as you think negatively, you'll never be able to choose a winning attitude. The second step is to identify your spouse's positive characteristics, even if that's difficult for you. You might even get help from your children by asking, "What are some of the good things about Daddy or Mommy?" Third, once you've identified those positive characteristics, thank God for them. Then, fourth, begin to express verbal appreciation to your spouse for the positive things you observe. Set a goal, such as giving one compliment a week for a month. Then move

3

toward two per week, then three, and so on until you're giving a compliment each day.

The book of Proverbs has a lot to say about the importance of words. Proverbs 18:21 says, "The tongue has the power of life and death" (NIV). Proverbs 12:18 talks about words bringing healing. Proverbs 15:4 calls gentle words "a tree of life." You can give your marriage new life when you replace condemnation and criticism with compliments and words of affirmation.

Lord God, thank you for all the wonderful things about my spouse. Please keep those fresh in my mind. Help me to use my words to acknowledge those things. May what I say heal and bring life.

Kindness

Be kind to each other, tenderhearted,
forgiving one another, just as God
through Christ has forgiven you.
EPHESIANS 4:32

"Be ye kind one to another" (Ephesians 4:32, KJV). We may have memorized it as children, but have we forgotten it as adults? In the Bible's famous "love chapter," kindness is defined as one of the traits of love: "Love is patient and kind" (1 Corinthians 13:4). Do you consciously think of being kind to your spouse throughout the day? Kindness is expressed in the way we talk as well as in what we do. Yelling and screaming are not kind. Speaking softly and respectfully is. So is taking the time to have a meaningful conversation with a spouse who is lonely, upset, or uncertain.

Then there are acts of kindness—things we do to help others. When we focus our energy on doing kind things for each other, our relationship can be rejuvenated. What could you do today to be kind to your spouse? Maybe it's taking on a chore that's not typically your responsibility, or bringing him or her a cup of coffee in bed. Or perhaps it's giving an encouraging note or bringing home a favorite treat. These are small things, but they can have a big impact. Imagine what your relationship would be like if you both emphasized kindness.

Lord Jesus, I want to show my love through kindness. Please help me to think of great ways today to be kind to the one I love.

Expressing Love

> Jesus replied, "The most important commandment is this: 'Listen, O Israel! The LORD our God is the one and only LORD. And you must love the LORD your God with all your heart, all your soul, all your mind, and all your strength.' The second is equally important: 'Love your neighbor as yourself.'"
>
> MARK 12:29-31

The word *Christian* means "Christlike." In the first century, *Christian* was not a name chosen by the followers of Jesus. Rather, it was a name given to them by others. Believers based their lifestyle on the teachings of Christ, so the best way to describe them was to call them Christians.

What if Christians really were Christlike? Central in Jesus' teachings is the command to love. In fact, in the verses above, Jesus said that the greatest commandment is to love God and the second is to love our neighbors. These commands supersede all others, because everything else flows out from them.

Love begins with an attitude, which in turn leads to acts of service. "How may I help you?" is a good question with which to begin. Today is a good day to express love to our neighbors. In my opinion, that starts with those closest to us—first our spouse, then our family—and then spreads outward.

Father, you made it clear that loving you and loving others is the most important thing I can do. Help me to make that a priority. Let me show Christlike love to my spouse today.

Division of Labor

Two people are better off than one, for they
can help each other succeed. If one person
falls, the other can reach out and help. But
someone who falls alone is in real trouble.

ECCLESIASTES 4:9-10

I vacuum the carpet and wash the dishes at my house. What do you do in your home? Who will do what? is a question that every couple must answer. In my opinion, the gifts and abilities of each person should be considered. One may be more qualified than the other for certain tasks. Why not use the player best qualified in that area?

This does not mean that once one person accepts a responsibility, the other will never offer to help with the task. Love seeks to help and often will. In Ecclesiastes, King Solomon wrote clearly about the value of teamwork. As a couple, we can accomplish more together than we could as two individuals because we are there to help each other. The Scriptures do not tell us exactly who should do what, but they do encourage us to agree on the answer.

The prophet Amos once asked, "Can two people walk together without agreeing on the direction?" (Amos 3:3). The answer is, "Not very far and not very well." I encourage you to keep negotiating until both of you feel good about who is doing what in your home.

Lord, thank you that my spouse and I can work as a team. Help us to find the best tasks for each of us, and help us to support each other as we work for the same goal.

Effective Apologies

> People who conceal their sins will not
> prosper, but if they confess and turn
> from them, they will receive mercy.
>
> PROVERBS 28:13

Effective apologies require a willingness to change our behavior. Proverbs 28:13 makes it clear that when we don't admit our wrongs—whether toward God or toward our spouse—we can't expect a good result. But when we do admit ("confess") the hurtful things we do and make a plan to stop doing them ("turn from them"), forgiveness is possible.

I remember Joel, whose wife, Joyce, was extremely negative. No matter what Joel said, Joyce disagreed with him. In our counseling sessions, I discovered that Joyce saw everything as either good or bad, right or wrong. Thus, if she disagreed with Joel, it couldn't just be a difference of opinion—his idea must be *wrong*.

It took a while, but eventually Joyce apologized for her negative attitude and came up with a plan to change it. She learned to say, "That's an interesting way to look at it." Or, "I can appreciate that." She learned to share her ideas as opinions rather than as dogma. She learned to say, "My perception of that is . . ." Joel freely forgave Joyce when he saw her genuinely trying to change. Effective apologies can save marriages.

God, it's hard to admit my own wrong patterns, but I know I hurt my spouse in the same way over and over again. Please give me the courage to confess those wrongs and turn away from them. And when my loved one does the same, help me to be gracious and to forgive.

Serving with Gladness

Make a joyful noise to the LORD, all the
earth! Serve the LORD with gladness!
Come into his presence with singing!

PSALM 100:1-2 (ESV)

A healthy marriage will include a positive attitude of
service between a husband and wife. She will want to
do things for him, and he will want to do things for
her. But how do you know what things to do? Simple:
You ask questions.

How about asking your spouse, "What is one thing
I could do for you this week that would make your life
easier?" When he or she tells you, you respond, "I'll try
to remember that." All true service must be given freely,
so the choice to do what your spouse suggests still rests
with you. But now you have a concrete idea of how to
invest your time and energy in a way that he or she will
appreciate.

When you choose to do what your spouse has
requested, you are serving Christ by serving your loved

one. The first verses of Psalm 100 remind us that we're called to serve with gladness. Serving God—whether directly or through serving others—can be joyful and energizing, and it can certainly bring blessing. It is the road to greatness, and it will also give you a growing marriage.

Father, I want to serve you with gladness. Help me to approach my spouse to find out how best to serve him or her—and then to do it with joy.

Sharing Money

I appeal to you, dear brothers and sisters, by
the authority of our Lord Jesus Christ, to live
in harmony with each other. Let there be no
divisions in the church. Rather, be of one
mind, united in thought and purpose.

1 CORINTHIANS 1:10

When you get married, it is no longer "your money"
and "my money" but rather "our money." Likewise, it
is no longer "my debts" and "your debts" but rather
"our debts." When you accept each other as partners,
you accept each other's liabilities as well as each other's
assets.

Before marriage, both partners should make a full
disclosure of their financial assets and liabilities. It is not
wrong to enter marriage with debts, but you ought to
know what those debts are, and you should agree on a
plan of repayment.

The motif of marriage is two becoming one. When
this is applied to finances, it implies that all your
resources belong to both of you. One of you may be

responsible for paying the bills and balancing the check-book, but this should never be used as an excuse for hiding financial matters from the other. One of you may have a higher salary, but that doesn't mean you get more say in how finances should be allocated.

Since the money belongs to both of you, both of you ought to agree on how it will be used. Full and open discussions should precede any financial decision, and agreement should be the goal. Follow the apostle Paul's advice and be "of one mind, united in thought and purpose." This is fitting for followers of Christ, whose priorities should be the same. Remember, you are partners, not competitors. Marriage is enhanced by agreement in financial matters.

Father God, thank you for making us one. Help us to strive for unity of purpose and priority when it comes to our money. May we be open and aboveboard in all our financial decisions.

Sharing Desires

Hope deferred makes the heart sick,
but a dream fulfilled is a tree of life.
PROVERBS 13:12

Now that we've looked at self-revelation, I want to talk about *sharing desires*. The failure to share desires is a source of much misunderstanding and frustration in any romantic relationship. Expecting your mate to fulfill your unexpressed desires is asking the impossible, and that makes disappointment inevitable. If you want your spouse to do something special on your birthday, for example, then say so. Don't expect your partner to read your mind.

In Proverbs 13:12, King Solomon presented a striking word picture of fulfilled and unfulfilled desires. Of course, not all our daily wishes rise to the level of making us heartsick if they're not fulfilled, but the basic idea is that when good, healthy desires are filled, joy can result.

Why wouldn't you want to do that for your spouse? And why wouldn't your spouse want that for you?

Letting your spouse know what you want is a vital part of self-revelation. Several statements reveal desires: "I want . . . ," "I wish . . . ," "Do you know what would really make me happy?" or "I'd like to . . ." If you express your desires, your spouse has a chance to accommodate them. You are not demanding; you are requesting. You cannot control your spouse's decisions. You can clearly state what you would like. It's a step toward intimacy.

Father, help me to communicate my desires more openly.
I don't want to be demanding, but I want to reveal more
of myself—and the things I hold close to my heart—
to the one I love. Please bless our relationship
as we strive to fulfill each other's desires.

The Peacemaker

God blesses those who work for peace,
for they will be called the children of God.

MATTHEW 5:9

If we are going to understand each other, we must identify our personality differences. There are many personality types, all of which have positives and negatives, and in the next few days we'll look at a few. Today we'll look at the peacemaker. This is the calm, slow, easygoing, well-balanced personality. This person is typically pleasant, doesn't like conflicts, seldom seems ruffled, and rarely expresses anger.

The peacemaker has emotions but does not easily reveal them. In a marriage, the peacemaker wants calm, tends to ignore disagreement, and avoids arguments at all costs. This person is very pleasant to be around; however, the downside of this personality is that conflicts are often left unresolved. If the couple does get into an argument, the peacemaker will try to calm the other person by acquiescing, even if he does not agree. He is kindhearted and sympathetic and wants everybody just to enjoy life. However, if a peacemaker is married to a controller, she may be steamrolled and eventually suffer in silent anger.

In the Sermon on the Mount, Jesus expressed blessing for the peacemakers and said that they will be called children of God. What a wonderful statement! James 3:18 gives a further accolade for this personality type: "Those who are peacemakers will plant seeds of peace and reap a harvest of righteousness." If you are married to a peacemaker, thank God for it. Also, be careful not to take advantage of your spouse's easygoing nature.

Father, I am thankful for my spouse's desire to be a peacemaker. I know that you bless this attitude. Please help me to appreciate it fully and not to use it for my own gain.

Laying the Groundwork of Teamwork

I planted the seed in your hearts, and Apollos
watered it, but it was God who made it grow. It's
not important who does the planting, or who does
the watering. What's important is that God makes
the seed grow. The one who plants and the one who
waters work together with the same purpose. And
both will be rewarded for their own hard work.
For we are both God's workers.

1 CORINTHIANS 3:6-9

Teamwork is the essential ingredient to a successful
marriage. Think about the first command God gave
Adam and Eve: to be fruitful and multiply. This command required teamwork; of course, neither a man nor a
woman can make a baby alone. As teamwork is required
in this basic biological goal, it is also required in the rest
of marriage.

The apostle Paul wrote about the concept of teamwork in 1 Corinthians 3. He was responding to some
new believers who were being divisive by proclaiming
their allegiance to either Paul or Apollos. He reminded
the Corinthians that it doesn't matter who completes

what task if both people have the same goal. He and Apollos both did their part to share the gospel, and they left the outcome in God's hands. That's teamwork.

The concept of teamwork is especially helpful when it comes to processing daily life. Cooking meals, washing dishes, paying bills, sweeping, mopping, mowing, trimming, and driving are all things that must be done to maintain life. Asking who is going to do what and how often will lead to teamwork. If you settle these issues early on, you will save yourselves a lot of conflict later. It's certainly undesirable to wake up months or years into the marriage and realize that you have spent a lot of time fighting when you could have spent it in productive activity.

Household tasks are not determined by gender. Some men are better cooks than their wives. Some women are better at math than their husbands and should handle the finances. You are teammates, not competitors. Why not work out a team plan that utilizes your best gifts? Remember: You're not enemies. You're on the same team.

Heavenly Father, it's easy for me to become competitive with my spouse. I'm concerned about who's doing more and focus too much on what is fair. Instead, show me how to be a good teammate. Help us to work together for the common goal of making our family run smoothly.

Handling Anger Constructively

Get rid of all bitterness, rage, anger, harsh words, and
slander, as well as all types of evil behavior. Instead,
be kind to each other, tenderhearted, forgiving one
another, just as God through Christ has forgiven you.
EPHESIANS 4:31-32

Learning how to handle your anger can be achieved
through a five-step process: (1) admit to yourself that
you are angry; (2) restrain your immediate response; (3)
locate the focus of your anger; (4) analyze your options;
and (5) take constructive action. Today we will focus
on step 5.

When you are angry with someone and need to
take constructive action, you have two basic choices.
The first is to lovingly confront the person with whom
you are angry. The second is to consciously decide to
overlook the matter. It's what the Bible calls forbearance. The book of Romans talks about God's mercy
and forbearance in not counting our sins against us.
Forbearance is the best option when you realize that
your anger is distorted and has grown out of selfishness.

If that's the case, you release your anger to God with a prayer: "Father, forgive me for being so selfish." Then you let it go. You may also choose to let go of offenses that are real but which you have blown out of proportion.

On the other hand, when your spouse has sinned against you, the clear biblical teaching is that you lovingly confront. "I realize I may not have all the facts, but I'm feeling angry and really need to talk with you. Is this a good time to talk?" Then you lay the matter before your spouse and seek reconciliation. In this case, anger has served a good purpose, and the relationship is restored.

Father, thank you that anger can serve a positive purpose.
Help us as a couple to move from anger to resolution,
so that our relationship may grow stronger.

Our Need to Love and Be Loved

How precious is your unfailing love, O God! All
humanity finds shelter in the shadow of your wings.

PSALM 36:7

Human behavior is motivated by certain physical, emotional, and spiritual needs. If you don't understand your
spouse's needs, you will never understand his or her
behavior.

The need to love and be loved is the most fundamental of our needs. The desire to love accounts for the
charitable side of humans. We feel good about ourselves
when we are loving others. On the other hand, much
of our behavior is motivated by the desire to *receive*
love. We feel loved when we are convinced that someone genuinely cares about our well-being. The psalm-
ist reiterates this human need to feel love in the verse
above when he thanks God for his unfailing love. The
image of people taking shelter in the Lord, like chicks

huddling under their mother's wings, touches us deeply because that need to be cared for is so significant.

When your spouse complains that you don't give her enough time, she is crying for love. When your spouse says, "I don't ever do anything right," he is begging for affirming words. Argue about the *behavior* and you will stimulate more negative behavior. Look *behind* the behavior to discover the emotional need. Meet that need, and you will eliminate the negative behavior. Love seeks to meet needs.

Father, please give me the maturity to look beyond my spouse's behavior to the need behind it. Help me to communicate my deep love to him or her.

Walking toward Reconciliation by Faith

Faith is the confidence that what we
hope for will actually happen; it gives us
assurance about things we cannot see.

HEBREWS 11:1

When things get tough in your marriage, it may seem easier to give up and pursue your own happiness, especially when the feelings of love have evaporated. However, the Christian's call is not to the easy road but to the right road. I can promise you that after the pain of reconciliation, the right road leads to both happiness and love.

The choice to pursue reconciliation is a step of faith. You cannot see the warmth of emotional love returning to your relationship. You cannot see differences being resolved. You cannot see the intimacy you desire in a marriage. Therefore, you must take the first steps by faith, not by sight. But it is not blind faith; it is faith based on the counsel of God. With your hand in God's hand, you must walk with him, trusting his wisdom that honoring the marriage covenant is the right thing to do.

When you step out in faith to seek reconciliation with your mate, you join the ranks of the biblical greats. Read Hebrews 11 for many examples of people who acted in faith, without any guarantees that things would go their way. The only assurance they had that things would ultimately turn out for the best was the promise of God. You have the same. Do you need more?

Father, I am challenged to step out in faith. When our marriage hits a rough spot, help me to work toward reconciliation because it's the right thing to do. I may not have any guarantees that my spouse will be receptive, but I have your promise to be with me. Please give me the strength to make the right choice.

Others above Self

Don't be concerned for your own good
but for the good of others.
1 CORINTHIANS 10:24

Most counselors agree that one of the greatest problems
in marriage is decision making. Visions of democracy
dance in the minds of many newly married couples,
but when there are only two voting members, democracy often results in deadlock. How does a couple move
beyond deadlock? The answer is found in one word:
love.

Love always asks the question, What is best for
you? As Paul wrote in 1 Corinthians, believers need
to be primarily concerned about what is beneficial
for others rather than just what will help or please
themselves. Love does not demand its own way. Love
seeks to bring pleasure to the one loved. That is why
Christians should have less trouble making decisions
than non-Christians. We are called to be lovers. When

I love my wife, I will not seek to force my will upon her for selfish purposes. Rather, I will consider what is in her best interests.

Putting my spouse, the one I love, above myself is such a simple concept, Lord, yet it's so difficult. I need your help. As we make decisions as a couple, help us not to demand but to offer. Help me to be loving in the way I make choices.

Covenant Marriage

Wherever you go, I will go; wherever you live,
I will live. Your people will be my people, and
your God will be my God. Wherever you die,
I will die, and there I will be buried.

RUTH 1:16-17

Is marriage a contract or a covenant? It's both, but the emphasis is on covenant. Why? Because most contracts apply to a limited amount of time—for example, a three-year contract to lease a car. Unfortunately, many people enter marriage with a contract mentality, thinking, *If it doesn't work, we can get a divorce.* Consequently, some research indicates that one-half of all marriages end within two years.

Covenants, on the other hand, are intended to be permanent, as we see in multiple places in the Bible. God made a covenant with Noah that extended to "all generations" (see Genesis 9). He did the same with Abraham (see Genesis 17). Covenants between two humans were also seen as permanent. For example, Ruth told her widowed mother-in-law, Naomi, that she would go wherever Naomi went and stay with her, adopting her culture and her religion, even until death. That beautiful statement of commitment is the language of covenant marriage. In fact, it's similar to what we say in most marriage ceremonies: "For better or for worse, for richer or for poorer, in sickness and in health, so long as we both shall live."

Christian marriage is viewed as a lifelong covenant. It is this commitment to marriage that helps us through the rough spots of life. If we have a contract mentality, then we bail out when things get tough. Perhaps it's time to remind yourself that you are committed to a covenant marriage.

Lord God, I am amazed that you entered into permanent covenants with sinful humans. You have made clear that marriage should be a permanent covenant as well. When my spouse and I are frustrated in our relationship, please remind us of our commitment. May it be an encouragement and a joy to us.

Encouraging a Quiet Person to Talk

Wise words bring many benefits, and hard work
brings rewards. . . . The wise listen to others.
PROVERBS 12:14-15

When it comes to talking, there are two personality
types. The first is what I call the Dead Sea personality. Just as the Dead Sea in Israel receives water from
the Jordan River but has no outlet, so many people
can receive all kinds of experiences throughout the day.
They store these in their minds and have little compul-
sion to share.

Then there is the personality that I call the Babbling
Brook. Whatever information comes in the eyes or ears
of this person quickly comes out the mouth. Often
these two types of people marry each other. Can they
have a happy marriage? Yes, if they understand their
personality differences and seek to grow.

Chances are the Babbling Brook will be complaining, "My mate won't talk. I don't ever know what he's

thinking. I feel like we are becoming strangers." How do you get a quiet person to talk?

Two suggestions: First, ask specific questions. The worst thing you can ever say to a Dead Sea personality is, "I wish you'd talk more." That statement is overwhelming, and it comes across as condemnation. It's far better to ask a specific question, because even the quietest person will generally respond.

Another suggestion is to stop the flow of your own words. If you want another person to talk more, you have to talk less. Leave little pools of silence. Remember, King Solomon wrote that "the wise listen to others." If you find yourself talking too much and your spouse talking too little, follow the advice of the apostle James and be "quick to listen, slow to speak" (James 1:19). Your marriage will benefit.

Heavenly Father, thank you for making my spouse and me so different. You know that one of us loves to talk and the other doesn't talk much without encouragement. Please help me to be quick to listen and to slow down my speech when I need to. I want to know my spouse better and to communicate more effectively with him or her.

Getting to Know You

You have searched me, LORD, and you know
me. You know when I sit and when I rise;
you perceive my thoughts from afar.

PSALM 139:1-2 (NIV)

Psalm 139 makes clear that God knows our every
thought and even our words before we speak them.
The Lord knows us—effortlessly—better than we know
ourselves. But it takes effort for a man and woman to
know each other. Do you see then why communication is an absolute necessity if we are to understand
our spouse?

We cannot know our spouse's thoughts, feelings, or
desires unless he or she chooses to tell us—and we choose
to listen. That is why a daily sharing time is so important
in a marriage. We cannot develop a sense of "togetherness" unless we talk regularly with each other.

A daily sharing time is a time set aside each day for
the purpose of talking and listening. If you're unsure
what to talk about, try this: "Tell me three things that

happened in your life today and how you feel about them." It can start with ten minutes and may extend to thirty or longer. The key is not the length but the consistency. I have never seen a truly successful marriage that did not *make* time for communication.

Father, I'm grateful that you know us inside and out. Help us to open ourselves to each other so we may grow in intimacy. Increase our oneness, Lord, we pray.

Love Brings Change

Above all, clothe yourselves with love,
which binds us all together in perfect harmony.
COLOSSIANS 3:14

Control is a significant issue in some relationships. One wife who was struggling with a controlling husband told me, "I feel like I'm a bird in a cage. Actually, I feel like a hamster in a cage—I don't have wings anymore. I don't want a divorce, but I don't know how much longer I can go on living under such pressure." This wife has lost her freedom and is feeling the pain of incarceration.

Is there hope? Yes, and it begins by believing that things can change. Can her husband change? Yes! Can she help stimulate that change? Yes! Her most powerful influence is love. The apostle Paul writes in Colossians 3 that we should seek love above all else. Why? Because love has the power to unite people, to bind them together even more closely. That's a powerful influence in a marriage.

In this woman's situation, two kinds of love are needed. First comes soft or tender love. She needs to learn to speak her husband's love language and seek to meet his need for emotional love. Second is tough love. She can say, "I love you too much to sit here and do nothing while you destroy our marriage." Then she must lay out some ground rules and consequences—in effect, tell him what she will do until he takes steps to change his behavior.

When a husband first feels tender love, he is then able to receive tough love.

Father, when I'm struggling in my marriage, help me to respond first with love. May my genuine, tender love speak to my spouse and clear the way for the necessary tough love to follow. Please guide me as I take these steps.

Seeking Companionship, Avoiding Loneliness

Live happily with the woman you love through
all the . . . days of life that God has given you
under the sun. The wife God gives you is
your reward for all your earthly toil.

ECCLESIASTES 9:9

One of the benefits of being married is companionship.
A loving, supportive spouse is not only good for your
emotional health, but also for your physical health.
Some time ago, a research project involving ten thousand married men, forty years of age or older, found
that those who had loving, supportive wives had signifi-
cantly fewer heart problems. An intimate relationship
in marriage enhances physical health.

However, loneliness within the marital relationship
is detrimental to health. Marriage is designed by God
to provide companionship. God said of Adam, "It is not
good for the man to be alone. I will make a helper who
is just right for him" (Genesis 2:18). Essentially, companions share life together. Thus, when a married couple

communicates with each other daily, they develop a sense of companionship. They are committed to each other. They stand together as they face the uncertainties of life. Something about having a companion makes life more bearable. That was God's plan. King Solomon wrote in Ecclesiastes that a wife—and, by extension, a husband—is a gift from God that refreshes us from the toil of daily life.

So as a couple, talk and listen to each other and build your relationship. Don't allow loneliness to rob your health.

Lord Jesus, thank you for the gift of marriage and the companionship it can bring. I want to bring friendship and partnership to my spouse, not loneliness. Please help us to strengthen our relationship more and more.

Parenting as a Team

As iron sharpens iron, so a friend sharpens a friend.
PROVERBS 27:17

Is it possible for two parents who have very different approaches to child-rearing to find a meeting of the minds? The answer is an unqualified yes. I've been there. In my marriage, we discovered that I tended to be the quiet, calm, "let's talk about it" parent. My wife, Karolyn, tended to be a "take action now" kind of parent. It took us a while to realize what was happening, analyze our patterns, and admit to each other our basic tendencies.

Eventually, though, we began to concentrate on the question, What is best for our children? We found that we could work together as a team and that, in fact, we must. Our basic tendencies did not change, but we did learn to temper them. I learned how to take responsible action and to blend words and actions. Karolyn learned to think before she moved.

The well-known proverb above is often applied to friendships or accountability groups. But it applies just as well—or better—to marriage. When we recognize that our spouse has different gifts and approaches that can balance ours, we are "sharpened." For those who have children, accepting our differences and learning how to complement each other makes for good parenting and a growing marriage.

Lord Jesus, thank you for the blessing of our children. I pray that you will help us to approach parenting as a couple. We have different approaches and strengths, and that's okay. Please give us the wisdom to blend those approaches in the best way and to work well as a team.

No Fear

Such love has no fear,
because perfect love expels all fear.
1 JOHN 4:18

Love is not our only emotional need, but it interfaces with all our other needs. We also need to feel secure, to have a healthy sense of self-worth, and to feel that our lives are significant. When two people choose to love each other, they also meet these needs. For example, if I know that my wife loves me, I feel secure in her presence.

The apostle John, who is known as "the disciple Jesus loved," writes a lot about love in his letters to believers. He wrote, "Perfect love casts out fear" (1 John 4:18, NKJV). In our relationship with God, this means that when we know the Lord loves us and has saved us, we are no longer afraid of judgment. In a sense, we can face anything. Genuine love in a human relationship has some of the same effects. Why should I be afraid if I am loved?

If I feel loved by my wife, then I also feel good about myself. After all, if she loves me, I must be worth loving. Ultimately, it is discovering that God loves me that gives me my greatest sense of worth. But my wife is an agent of God's love.

If my spouse loves me, I'm also more likely to feel that my life has significance. We want our lives to count for something; we want to make a difference in the world. When we give love to and receive love from our spouse, we *are* making a difference. We are enriching his or her life. This is what God called us to do—express his love in the world. Why not start at home?

Father, I want to make a difference—and I know I can start at home by loving my spouse. May my love be so strong and genuine that it changes the way he or she feels about life. May I always understand that my true worth comes because of your love.

Meeting Emotional Needs

Husbands ought to love their wives as their own
bodies. He who loves his wife loves himself.
EPHESIANS 5:28 (NIV)

Meeting my wife's emotional need for love is a choice
I make every day. If I know her primary love language
and choose to speak it, her deepest emotional need will
be met, and she will feel secure in my love. If she does
the same for me, my emotional needs are met, and both
of us live with a full "love tank."

In this state of emotional contentment, both of us
can give our creative energies to many wholesome proj-
ects outside the marriage while we continue to keep our
relationship exciting and growing.

How do you create this kind of marriage? It all
begins with the choice to love. I recognize that God
has given me, as a husband, the responsibility of meeting my wife's need for love. Paul's words in Ephesians 5
make that clear. I am not only to love my wife, but

to love her as I love my own body. That's a tall order, but with the Holy Spirit's help, I choose to accept that responsibility. Then I learn how to speak her primary love language, and I choose to speak it regularly. What happens? My wife's attitude and feelings toward me become positive. Now she reciprocates, and my need for love is also met. Love is a choice.

Heavenly Father, you have given us high standards for loving each other. We need your help to make the right choices to love. Please refresh us with your Holy Spirit and rejuvenate our relationship.

Dealing with Yourself First

> Why worry about a speck in your friend's eye when you have a log in your own? How can you think of saying to your friend, "Let me help you get rid of that speck in your eye," when you can't see past the log in your own eye? Hypocrite! First get rid of the log in your own eye; then you will see well enough to deal with the speck in your friend's eye.
>
> MATTHEW 7:3-5

It is important that we take responsibility for our own failures, rather than blaming our spouse. But that doesn't mean we should never discuss our mate's shortcomings. As a couple, we are trying to learn how to work together as a team. This means that if I think my spouse is treating me unfairly, I should, in love, share my feelings. But that's only appropriate after I have first dealt with my own failures.

This is what Jesus taught in the verses above from Matthew 7. When we cast blame on our mate without first examining ourselves, we're likely not seeing past our own faults—and as a result, it becomes impossible to see the problem clearly. Whenever a relationship breaks down, both people are a part of the breakdown. One may bear more responsibility than the other, but either can move to restore the relationship. We must each deal with the wrong we personally bear.

Be willing to take the first step. Don't sit around blaming your spouse, and don't waste time waiting for him or her to confess. If you honestly confess your part, that may be the stimulus that triggers confession on the part of your mate. The first step is the most important one.

Father, I pray for the humility and courage to take the first step. Help me to see the wrong I have contributed to a situation and confess that, without waiting for my spouse to act first. Please bless our efforts.

Learning Affirmation

Dear brothers and sisters, I close my letter with these
last words: Be joyful. Grow to maturity. Encourage
each other. Live in harmony and peace. Then
the God of love and peace will be with you.

2 CORINTHIANS 13:11

Today, I want to give two guidelines for learning to
speak affirming words. First, *don't give backhanded
encouragement*. That is, don't smother your comments
in sarcasm. For example, "It took you almost two whole
days to finish that bag of Oreos. I admire your will-
power." It should go without saying, but comments like
these are not affirming. Leave off the "zingers" if you
want to affirm.

Second, *don't get upset if your spouse's response
doesn't live up to your expectations*. Remember, everyone
responds to compliments in a different way. Sure, it
would be great if your spouse responded to your affirmation with a smile and a hug, but you may get that
"What are you talking about?" look instead. This is
especially true if you and your spouse are new to the

affirmation business. The good news is that the more you give compliments, the better response you'll get.

At the end of 2 Corinthians, Paul gives a list of short directives to his listeners. Right in the midst of those is encouraging each other. It's a biblical mandate, it's something that pleases God, and it will strengthen your marriage. Take your first step today.

Father, thank you for the encouragement I receive from your Word. Please help me as I seek to change my words from negative to positive. Show me the best way to affirm my spouse so that he or she may be encouraged and feel sure of my love.

Focused Attention

Love each other with genuine affection,
and take delight in honoring each other.
ROMANS 12:10

It has been my observation that many husbands simply do not understand the needs of their wives. Some husbands believe that if they work a steady job and bring home a decent salary, they have fulfilled their role as husband. They have little concept of a wife's emotional and social needs. Consequently, they make no effort to meet those needs. (I can hear some of you wives saying, "Yes!" as you read this.)

But I have also observed that many wives do not understand their husbands' needs. Some wives believe that if they take care of the children and work with their husbands to keep food on the table and keep the house in some semblance of order, they are being good wives. They have little concept of their husbands' need for admiration and affection.

Often, it's just a matter of focus. Why is it that when we were dating, we focused so much time and attention on each other, but after a few years of marriage, we focus on everything else? The fact is, we desperately need each other. The Bible calls us not only to love each other but to take delight in it! I want to call you to refocus attention on your spouse.

Father, you know how much my spouse and I need each other. You created us that way. Please help us to be aware of each other's needs and to take delight in meeting them.

Total Commitment

Fear the LORD and serve him wholeheartedly. Put
away forever the idols your ancestors worshiped
when they lived beyond the Euphrates River
and in Egypt. Serve the LORD alone.

JOSHUA 24:14

Most women have an emotional need for security. It is
first a physical need—to be safe from danger inside and
outside of the home—but her greatest security need
is often for assurance that her husband is committed
to her.

The husband who threatens his wife with divorce
or makes offhanded comments such as, "You'd be better
off with someone else" or "I think I'll find someone
else," is playing into a dysfunctional pattern.

When Joshua was leading the Israelites to the
Promised Land, he challenged them to be totally com-
mitted to the Lord. They could no longer serve the
God of Israel and still try to worship their old idols.
They needed to make a choice. We face a similar ques-
tion when we come to marriage. Will we put aside any

thoughts or comments about divorce and be totally committed to our spouse?

The wise husband will make every effort to communicate to his wife that whatever happens, he is with her. If there are disagreements, he will take the time to listen, understand, and seek resolution. If she suffers physical or emotional pain, he will be by her side. Every wife should be able to say, "I know that my husband is with me, no matter what happens. He is committed to our marriage." Every husband needs the same commitment from his wife.

Lord God, I know that I need to be totally committed to my spouse. He or she is a gift that you have given me, and I am thankful. Please help me to show my commitment through my words and my actions so my spouse will feel secure in my support.

Focusing on the Goal

Look straight ahead, and fix your eyes on
what lies before you. Mark out a straight path
for your feet; stay on the safe path. Don't get
sidetracked; keep your feet from following evil.

PROVERBS 4:25-27

Ironic, isn't it, that with all the "time savers" of modern
technology, we seem to have even less time for each
other? Microwaves, remote controls, dishwashers, and
computers were supposed to save us valuable time. But
what happened to all that extra time? Apparently, it got
gobbled up by other activities. Can we reclaim some of
that time for our marriages? The answer is yes, *if* we set
goals and make time to reach those goals.

The passage above from Proverbs 4 shows King
Solomon's advice for meeting goals. Essentially, it comes
down to knowing where you're going, setting a straight
path to get there, and not getting sidetracked. That's
the approach we need to take if we're going to meet our
goals for marriage.

How do we make time? By eliminating some of

the good things we are doing so that we will have time for the best. Life's meaning is not found in money, sports, shopping, academic success, or career achievement, as good as some of those things are. It is found in relationships—first with God, and then with people. If you are married, nothing is more important than your marital relationship. It is the framework in which God wants you to invest your life and experience his love. The husband is told to "love" his wife, and she is instructed to "honor" him. How better to love and honor than to make time for each other?

Father, thank you for the goals we've been able to set for our relationship. I pray for the wisdom and self-control to keep looking straight ahead at the goal. Let us not be distracted by other things that could keep us from meeting our goal, even if they're good things. Please show us how to straighten out our priorities.

Modeling Spiritual Hunger

When we get together, I want to encourage you in
your faith, but I also want to be encouraged by yours.

ROMANS 1:12

How do you develop spiritual intimacy in your relationship? One wife said to me, "I wish that my husband
and I could share more about spiritual things. He seems
willing to talk about everything else, but when I men-
tion church, God, or the Bible, he clams up and walks
away. I don't know what to do, but it's very frustrating."
What advice would you give this wife?

Here's what I said: "Don't ever stop talking about
spiritual things. Your relationship with God is the most
important part of your life. If you don't share this part
of yourself, your husband will never know who you are.
However, don't expect him to reciprocate, and don't
preach him a sermon until he asks for one. Simply share
what God is doing in your life. Share a Scripture that

helped you make a decision or encouraged you when you were feeling down.

"When you share what your spiritual life is like, you stimulate hunger. When your husband gets spiritually hungry, he will likely want to discuss things with you. At that point, spiritual intimacy will begin."

Encouraging each other in our faith is a valuable goal. Even the apostle Paul wanted to be encouraged by seeing the faith of the Roman believers. When we reach the point of sharing our spiritual successes and struggles, our marriage will be blessed.

Father, please help me to be patient with my spouse when he or she does not want to discuss spiritual things. I pray that you would work in our hearts and bring us closer together in this area. Develop our relationships with you as well as our spiritual intimacy with each other.

Making Decisions Together

Trust in the LORD with all your heart; do not depend
on your own understanding. Seek his will in all you
do, and he will show you which path to take.

PROVERBS 3:5-6

Can we develop a method of decision-making that
doesn't include arguing? I think the answer is yes, but
this doesn't imply dictatorship. The husband who rules
with a "rod of iron" or the wife who insists on having the last word might get compliance, but they will
not attain unity. Unity requires that we treat each other
with respect. We understand that we will not always
agree, but when we disagree, we will respect each other's
ideas, even if we don't fully understand them.

"Two people are better off than one," the Bible says
(Ecclesiastes 4:9), but how can that be apparent if one
person acts alone? Most of the poor decisions made
in marriages are made in isolation. If I make a decision without consulting my wife, I am limited to my
own wisdom. How tragic. God instituted marriage as a

partnership where two people work together as a team. When we pool our wisdom, we are far more likely to make a wise decision.

The Bible clearly instructs us not to depend, or "lean," on our own limited understanding, as we see in Proverbs 3. Certainly, as couples, above all we need to ask God for wisdom as we make decisions. As we do that, both partners' insights are necessary and valuable.

Life is hard. Why go it alone? Treat your spouse as a valued partner. Recognize that God gave you a wealth of wisdom when he gave you a spouse.

Father, thank you for the gift of my spouse and for the wisdom he or she represents. When we make decisions, please keep me from either taking over or abdicating all responsibility. Help us to talk together, reason well, and make wise decisions.

Working for Change

Anyone who belongs to Christ has become a new
person. The old life is gone; a new life has begun!

2 CORINTHIANS 5:17

Living with an irresponsible spouse is not fun. However,
watching an irresponsible spouse change and grow can
be great fun. The first step to encouraging this change is
to find out why your spouse is irresponsible; but I want
to suggest that the next step is ackowledging your own
failures in the past.

If you want to see change in your spouse, it is always
best to begin by changing yourself. You know, and your
spouse knows, that you have not been perfect. When you
confess your own failures to yourself, to God, and then to
your spouse, you are paving the road to growth for both
of you. The apostle Paul makes clear in 2 Corinthians
5:17 that those who belong to Christ are beginning new
lives. Never forget that God has the power to transform
your own heart as well as your spouse's. When you begin

with what you can control—yourself—and ask God to change you, changes in your spouse will not be far behind.

Consider saying this to your spouse: "I know I've been critical of you. I've realized that in many ways I have failed to be the Christian spouse I should have been. I know I haven't always given you the encouragement you needed. I hope that you will forgive me. I want the future to be different." With that communication, you have immediately changed the climate between the two of you. You have opened the door to growth.

Lord, I am grateful that you are in the business of changing lives. Though it's tempting to think that only my spouse needs to change, I know that's not true. Please help me to be willing to change as well. Show me how to be a better partner and grant me the humility to confess my wrongs to my spouse without first demanding change from him or her.

Having the Attitude of Christ

You must have the same attitude that Christ
Jesus had. Though he was God, he did not think
of equality with God as something to cling to.
Instead, he gave up his divine privileges; he took
the humble position of a slave and was born as
a human being. When he appeared in human
form, he humbled himself in obedience to
God and died a criminal's death on a cross.

PHILIPPIANS 2:5-8

How does my relationship with God affect my marriage? Profoundly! By nature, I'm self-centered. I carry that attitude into my marriage. So, when I don't get my way, I argue or sulk. That doesn't lead to a growing marriage. My attitude must change, and that's where God comes into the picture. He is in the business of changing attitudes.

The apostle Paul says, "You must have the same attitude that Christ Jesus had." What was his attitude? He was willing to step from heaven to earth to identify with us—something that one translation describes as "becoming nothing." Once he became a man, he was willing to step down even further and die for us. Jesus' attitude is first and foremost an attitude of sacrificial love and service. If that attitude is in me, I will have a growing marriage.

My research has shown that not a single wife in the history of this nation has ever murdered her husband while he was washing the dishes. Not one! That's a bit tongue-in-cheek, but it ought to tell us something.

Developing this attitude of service may seem impossible, but it's not. Never underestimate God's power to transform a willing individual.

Lord Jesus, I am amazed at your attitude of humble
servanthood. I can't even understand what it must
have been like for you to set aside so much to become a
limited human—and to die for us. Thank you, Lord.
I need your transformation to have this same attitude.
Please give me a willing heart.

Admitting Mistakes

Where there is no counsel, the people fall; but in
the multitude of counselors there is safety.
PROVERBS 11:14 (NKJV)

"You're the one with the problem. I don't need counseling." Have you ever heard this? The person who thinks
he's always right is mistaken. No one is perfect. We all
need help. The book of Proverbs says that "in the multitude of counselors there is safety." Why? Because other
people can often bring clearer perspective to our problems. The person who refuses to seek counsel and tries
to handle things on his own is often insecure. He thinks
that to admit that he made a mistake is to prove that he
is inadequate, and that is his greatest fear. Perhaps his
father told him he would never make it, and he is trying
hard to prove his father wrong.

How can you help, if you are married to this person? Give unconditional love. Speak her primary love
language often. Brag on her in front of your friends,

both in her presence and behind her back. Focus on her accomplishments. When she knows she is secure in your love, perhaps she will be able to admit that she's not perfect. When she does, let her know how much you admire her for admitting her failures. When she sees that her success is not dependent on being perfect, she can relax and become the person God has made her to be.

Father, it's sometimes hard for me to admit my own mistakes. Please help me to realize that pretending I'm perfect doesn't make the problems go away but just makes things worse. When my spouse struggles with this, show me how to respond lovingly in a way that builds him or her up. Help me to love unconditionally, not based on what he or she does.

Following God's Example of Teamwork

> God decided in advance to adopt us into his own
> family by bringing us to himself through Jesus
> Christ. This is what he wanted to do, and it gave
> him great pleasure. . . . And when you believed in
> Christ, he identified you as his own by giving you
> the Holy Spirit, whom he promised long ago.
>
> EPHESIANS 1:5, 13

It seems to me that if we could understand God better, we could understand marriage better. Ever notice how God the Father, God the Son, and God the Holy Spirit work together as a team? Read the first chapter of Ephesians and observe how the Father planned our salvation, the Son shed his blood to effect our salvation, and the Holy Spirit sealed our salvation. God is one within the mystery of the Trinity, and this unity is expressed in the diversity of roles needed to accomplish one goal, our salvation.

The Scriptures say that, in marriage, the husband and wife are to become one flesh. However, this unity does not mean that we are clones of each other. No, we are two distinct creatures who work together as a team to accomplish one goal—God's will for our lives. In mundane things such as washing clothes and mopping floors, or in exciting things such as volunteering in a soup kitchen or leading a Bible study, we complement each other. The husband who takes care of the children while his wife leads a Bible study is sharing with her in ministry. Indeed, two become one when they work together as a team.

Father, I am grateful for your example of teamwork. I can't fully understand the Trinity, but I know that your three persons work together in perfect unity. I pray for that kind of unity within my relationship with my spouse. Help us to function smoothly as a team, being generous with each other and keeping our end goal in mind. May our marriage glorify you as we do your will.

Touch to Comfort

> For everything there is a season, a time for every
> activity under heaven. . . . A time to cry and a time
> to laugh. A time to grieve and a time to dance. A
> time to scatter stones and a time to gather stones.
> A time to embrace and a time to turn away.
>
> ECCLESIASTES 3:1, 4-5

Almost instinctively in a time of crisis, we hug one another. Why? In a crisis, more than anything, we need to feel loved. We cannot always change events, but we can survive if we feel loved.

All marriages will experience crises. The death of parents is inevitable. Automobile accidents injure thousands each year. Disease is no respecter of persons. Disappointments are a part of life. The most important thing you can do for your spouse in a time of crisis is to love him or her. Especially if your spouse's primary love language is physical touch, nothing is more important than holding her as she cries or putting a hand on his shoulder as he makes a difficult decision. Your words may mean little to a person who is hurt or in shock, but your physical touch will communicate that you care.

Ecclesiastes 3 reminds us that there's a time for everything, and crises provide unique opportunities for expressing love. Tender touches will be remembered long after the crisis has past, but your failure to touch may never be forgotten. Physical touch is a powerful love language. In a time of crisis, a hug is worth more than a thousand words.

Heavenly Father, when we face a difficult situation as a couple, help me to reach out to my spouse with loving touch. May my touch bring comfort.

Breaking the Silence

Be an example to all believers in what you say, in the
way you live, in your love, your faith, and your purity.

1 TIMOTHY 4:12

When your spouse gives you the "silent treatment," you
may feel helpless. But you're not. You can help break
the silence. However, you don't do it by criticizing your
spouse for not talking. Instead, you do it by trying to
understand what is going on inside your loved one and
addressing those issues.

I can hear someone saying, "But how can I know
what is going on inside him if he won't talk?" The answer
is to *think*. Think about your spouse's emotional needs.
When our emotional needs are not met, we act badly,
and silence is one form the misbehavior can take.

Jill addressed the issue when she said to her husband, "Mike, I realize that I have not been speaking your
love language lately. I'm sorry about that. I got so busy
that I forgot the main thing—I love you. I think that

your silence is probably related to the fact that you feel neglected by me. If so, could we agree that next time this happens, you will simply say, 'My love tank is empty. I need to know that you love me'? I promise you I'll respond, because I do love you."

You guessed it. In response to that loving, honest request, Mike started talking. As 1 Timothy 4:12 mentions, our words should be above reproach, and our love should be evident. When that's the case, we will have a positive effect on others.

Lord, please give me the maturity, the self-control, and the wisdom to respond lovingly to my spouse when he or she has stopped talking to me. Show me how to address the core issue of his or her emotional needs. Heal our relationship.

Studying Your Spouse

The husband should fulfill his wife's sexual needs,
and the wife should fulfill her husband's needs.
1 CORINTHIANS 7:3

We must understand male-female differences if we
are going to discover God's ideal for sexual intimacy.
The husband's emphasis is most often on the physical
aspects: the seeing, the touching, the feeling. The wife,
on the other hand, typically emphasizes the emotional
aspect. Feeling loved, cared for, and treated tenderly will
pave the road to sexual intimacy for her.

The apostle Paul's words make clear that as a
couple, our goal must be to meet each other's sexual
needs. That takes some deliberate work. The husband
must learn to focus on his wife's emotional need for
love. The wife must understand the physical and visual
aspect of her husband's sexual desires. As in all other
areas of marriage, this requires learning. If the couple
focuses on making the sexual experience an act of love,

each seeking to pleasure the other, they will find fulfilling sexual intimacy. But if they simply "do what comes naturally," they will find sexual frustration.

It should be obvious that we cannot separate sexual intimacy from emotional, intellectual, social, and spiritual intimacy. We can study them separately, but in the context of human relationships, they can never be compartmentalized.

The sense of closeness, of being one, of finding mutual satisfaction is reserved for the couple who is willing to do the hard work of learning about each other. Love can be learned, and sexual intimacy is one of the results.

Lord Jesus, it's easy to fall into selfishness when it comes to sex. As a couple, please help us to focus on each other. May our desire to please each other increase, and may that strengthen our relationship.

Intercessory Prayer

I pray for you constantly, asking God, the
glorious Father of our Lord Jesus Christ, to give
you spiritual wisdom and insight so that you
might grow in your knowledge of God.

EPHESIANS 1:16-17

Martin Luther said, "As it is the business of tailors to
make clothes and cobblers to mend shoes, so it is the
business of Christians to pray." Intercession is one ministry that requires no special spiritual gift. All Christians
are equipped to pray.

Not only is intercessory prayer a ministry, it is also
a responsibility. The prophet Samuel told the Israelites,
"I will certainly not sin against the LORD by ending my
prayers for you" (1 Samuel 12:23). The apostle Paul
began many of his epistles by telling his readers how fre-
quently he prayed for them. Prayer is one of the means
that God has chosen to let us cooperate with him in getting his work done. It is a ministry that husbands and
wives can do together. They can pray for each other as

well as for their children, their parents, their pastor and church, other ministries, and world missions.

If you don't have a daily prayer time with your spouse, why not start today? Ask your spouse to spend five minutes praying with you. If you don't want to pray out loud, then pray silently. Take the first step in learning the ministry of intercessory prayer.

Heavenly Father, your Word makes clear how important prayer is. I want to lift up my spouse, my family, and others to you meaningfully and often. Please help us as a couple to develop good habits of prayer. As we pray together, may that shared experience and our shared desires for your will to be done draw us closer together.

Choosing Love

Now I am giving you a new commandment:
Love each other. Just as I have loved you,
you should love each other.

JOHN 13:34

The Five Love Languages, a book I wrote several years ago, has helped hundreds of thousands of couples rediscover warm feelings for each other. Now, this did not happen because someone decided, "I'm going to have warm feelings toward my spouse again." It began when one person decided, "I'm going to express love to my spouse *in spite of the fact* that I don't have warm feelings toward him or her." That person learned the love language that spoke most deeply to his or her spouse and spoke it regularly.

What happened? The person who was receiving such love began to have warm feelings toward the spouse who was loving. In time, the recipient reciprocated and learned to speak the other's love language. Now they both have warm feelings for each other.

Emotional love can be rediscovered. The key is learning your spouse's love language and choosing to speak it regularly. Warm feelings result from loving actions. Jesus commanded his disciples—and, by extension, all believers—to love each other as he loved them. His love is not measured in warm feelings, although I have no doubt those are present. Rather, we know Jesus loves us because of what he did for us. Love is a choice, and when we make that choice, we emulate our Savior.

Lord Jesus, thank you for loving me so much that you died on the cross to save me. You are the ultimate example of love. Please help me to make the choice to love my spouse. As I act lovingly, I know that loving feelings will come.

Accepting Responsibility

We are each responsible for our own conduct.

GALATIANS 6:5

Why are we so quick to blame our loved one when things aren't going well in our relationship? Unfortunately, it's human nature, going all the way back to Adam and Eve. (See Genesis 3 for some blatant blame-shifting between the two of them.) But Galatians 6:5 reminds us that each of us is responsible for our own choices and behavior, and that includes our part in a relationship.

May I suggest a better approach? Try the following steps:

1. I realize that my marriage is not what it should be.
2. I stop blaming my mate and ask God to show me where I am at fault.
3. I confess my sin and accept God's forgiveness, according to 1 John 1:9.

4. I ask God to fill me with his Spirit and give me the power to make constructive changes in my life.
5. I go to my mate, confess my failures, and ask forgiveness.
6. In God's power, I go on to change my behavior, words, and attitudes, according to the principles that I discover in Scripture.

This is God's plan, and it works. Blaming your spouse stimulates resentment and antagonism. Admitting your own failures and letting God change your behavior creates a new and positive climate in your marriage. It is the road to a growing marriage.

Father, you know how easily I slip into blaming my spouse for the things that are wrong in our relationship. Please forgive me. Help me instead to take full responsibility for my own wrongs. Show me clearly where I have failed, and help me to change. I know I can do it only in your power.

Speaking Another's Love Language

Let love be your highest goal!
1 CORINTHIANS 14:1

What if speaking your spouse's love language doesn't come naturally for you? The answer is simple: You *learn* to speak it.

My wife's love language is acts of service. One of the things I do regularly for her as an act of love is to vacuum the house. Do you think that vacuuming floors comes naturally for me? When I was a kid, my mother made me vacuum. On Saturdays, I couldn't play ball until I vacuumed the whole house. In those days, I said to myself, *If I ever get out of here, there's one thing I'm never going to do: vacuum!*

You couldn't pay me enough to vacuum the house. There is only one reason I do it: *love*. You see, when an action doesn't come naturally to you, doing it is a greater expression of love. My wife knows that every time I vacuum the house, it's nothing but 100 percent pure, unadulterated love, and I get credit for the whole thing. The Bible reminds us that love should be our highest goal. We can make it an attainable goal by speaking our spouse's love language, even when it's not our own.

And how do I benefit? I get the pleasure of living with a wife who has a full love tank. What a way to live!

Father God, you know that sometimes my spouse's love language doesn't feel natural to me. Please help me to do it anyway—and to do it completely because of love.

Helpful Words

The lips of the godly speak helpful words.
PROVERBS 10:32

Distorted anger is the kind of anger you feel when the person you love disappoints you. One way to deal with it is something I call "negotiating understanding." If you're feeling anger or hurt, it needs to be processed with your spouse in a positive way.

Here's an example. You might begin by saying, "I want to share something with you that is not designed in any way to put you down. I love you, and I want our relationship to be open and genuine, so I feel that I must share some of the struggles I'm having. Over the past few months, I've sometimes felt hurt, disappointed, and neglected. A lot of it focuses around your going to the gym three nights a week. Please understand that I'm not against your efforts to stay in shape. I'm not even asking you to change that. I just want you to know what I'm feeling. Hopefully we can find an answer together."

Those are helpful words and show that your primary goal is finding a solution, not being right. According to Proverbs 10:32, the godly speak helpful words like this. So, when you take this approach, you're acting in a way God approves. Such an open, positive approach creates a setting for the two of you to negotiate understanding and find a growing marriage.

Lord God, I want my words to be helpful, not hurtful. As we discuss issues as a couple, please give us the desire to find a solution together. Help me to give up the need to be right.

Expressing Regret

I confess my sins; I am deeply
sorry for what I have done.

PSALM 38:18

There are multiple languages of apology, and one is
regret. Apology is birthed in the womb of regret. We
regret the pain we have caused, the disappointment,
the inconvenience, the betrayal of trust. The offended
person wants some evidence that we realize how deeply
we have hurt him or her. For some people, this is the
one thing they listen for in an apology. Without the
expression of regret, they do not sense that the apology
is adequate.

A simple "I'm sorry" can go a long way toward
restoring goodwill, but that kind of apology has more
impact when it is specific. For what are you sorry? "I'm
sorry that I was late. I know that you pushed yourself to
get here on time and then I was not here. I know how
frustrating that can be. I feel bad that I did this to you.

The problem was that I didn't start on time. I hope you can forgive me and we can still have a good evening."

Including details reveals the depth of your understanding of the situation and how much you inconvenienced your spouse. When we confess our sins to God, as in the psalm above, we are usually specific about the wrongs we have committed and sincere in expressing our sorrow. We should extend that kind of apology to our spouse as well.

Father, I know that when my spouse expresses sincere regret, it makes a huge difference in how I perceive his or her apology. Please help me to extend that kind of apology to him or her as well so that we can deal with the wrongs between us.

Accepting Worthwhile Advice

"This is not good!" Moses' father-in-law exclaimed.
. . . "This job is too heavy a burden for you to handle
all by yourself. . . . Select from all the people some
capable, honest men who fear God and hate bribes.
Appoint them as leaders." . . . Moses listened to his
father-in-law's advice and followed his suggestions.

EXODUS 18:17-18, 21, 24

When we marry, we commit to leaving our parents and
cleaving to our spouse. But leaving parents does not
mean that we will not consider their suggestions. After
all, our parents are older than we are, and perhaps wiser.
Your parents or in-laws may have some good advice.

In the book of Exodus, we see that Moses was an
overworked administrator until he took the advice
of his father-in-law. Jethro observed Moses spending
hours judging all the Israelites' disagreements and suggested that Moses was on the fast track to burnout.
When he shared the principle of *delegation*, Moses said
to himself, *Why didn't I think of that?* That night he
talked with his wife about the idea and the next day

posted a sign outside his office: *Help Wanted*. Well, not exactly. But he did appoint several managers, to whom he delegated much of his work. It was one of the best decisions Moses ever made, and he got the idea from his father-in-law.

In following Jethro's advice, Moses demonstrated his own maturity. He did not feel compelled to rebel against a good idea simply because it came from his father-in-law. He didn't feel the need to prove his own intelligence. Rather, he was secure enough in his own self-worth that he could accept a good idea, regardless of its source. I hope that you will be as wise as Moses.

Lord Jesus, thank you for the wisdom and experience you have given my parents and my parents-in-law. You know how easy it is for me to discount their suggestions. When they give good advice, please show me how to accept it graciously.

Fostering Oneness

I want [believers] to be encouraged and
knit together by strong ties of love.

COLOSSIANS 2:2

The Scriptures indicate that husbands and wives are
to become "one" (see Genesis 2:24). They are to share
life to such a degree that they have a sense of unity,
or togetherness. In the verse above, the apostle Paul
states his vision for believers: that they would be "knit
together" or "united in love" (NIV). This is critical for
all believers and even more so for marriage partners.
Would you describe your marriage like this?

"We are a team."
"We know each other."
"We understand each other."
"We choose to walk in step with each other."
"Our lives are inseparably bound together."
"We are one."

These are the statements of happily married couples. Such togetherness does not happen without a lot of communication. Communication is a two-way street. I talk and you listen; you talk and I listen. It is this simple process that develops understanding and togetherness.

How much time do you spend in conversation with your spouse each day? Do you have a daily sharing time? How consistent are you in keeping this appointment? Intentional, daily conversations can enhance communication and increase oneness.

Lord Jesus, I know you desire us to be united as a couple. I pray that we will grow in togetherness, in team-work, in understanding, and in our sense of oneness. Please show us how to do that.

Joy through Service

The commandments of the LORD are right,
bringing joy to the heart. The commands of
the LORD are clear, giving insight for living.

PSALM 19:8

What if your significant other's love language is acts of service? What if you discover that the thing that really makes her feel loved is your taking out the garbage, washing the dishes, or doing the laundry? One husband said, "I'd say that she is probably not going to feel loved." Well, that's one approach, but the more biblical approach is to learn to serve your spouse.

It may not be easy for you to learn to speak the language of acts of service. I remember one wife who told me, "I'll have to admit, there were some trying and humorous times in those early weeks when my husband began to help me around the house. The first time he did the laundry, he used undiluted bleach instead of regular detergent. Our blue towels came out with white polka dots. But he was loving me in my language, and my love tank was filling up. Now he knows how to do everything around the house and is always helping me. We have much more time together because I don't have to work all the time. Believe me, I have learned to speak his love language too. We are a happy couple."

The Lord loves it when we serve each other in love and put each other's needs above our own. When we follow his commands, joy often follows—as mentioned in the psalm above and as evident in this couple's example. Learn to speak your spouse's love language, and you, too, can have a growing, thriving relationship.

Father, following your commands brings joy. Thank you for the love and rejuvenation that can come when we serve each other and communicate love to each other. I pray for the grace to do that willingly.

The Cure for Loneliness

Two people lying close together can keep each
other warm. But how can one be warm alone? A
person standing alone can be attacked and defeated,
but two can stand back-to-back and conquer.

ECCLESIASTES 4:11-12

There are two types of loneliness: emotional and social.
Even in marriage we can experience both.

Emotional loneliness is not feeling close to your
spouse. You feel like you and your mate don't really
know each other. *Social loneliness* is the feeling of isolation that comes when you and your spouse have no
shared activities. You don't do anything together.

The cure to emotional loneliness comes not from
cursing the darkness but from initiating conversation.
Start with simple questions: "Did you eat anything exciting today?" "What was the best moment of your day?"
Move to more important questions: "When you think of
the future, what could I do to enhance your life?"

The cure to social loneliness is to initiate activities
together. Rather than complaining that you don't ever

do anything together, plan something that you think your spouse would enjoy, and invite him or her to join you. Positive action is always better than negative complaints. The journey of a thousand miles begins with one step—and it is a worthwhile journey. As the book of Ecclesiastes reminds us, there are many reasons why two are better than one. Embrace that concept and seek out deeper companionship with your spouse.

Lord God, I am encouraged by these ideas of things to do to combat the loneliness I feel. Help me to initiate conversations and activities that will bring my spouse and me closer together. I want to take the first step. Thank you for creating us to be companions.

Balancing Work and Family

Live happily with the woman you love through
all the . . . days of life that God has given you
under the sun. The wife God gives you is
your reward for all your earthly toil.

ECCLESIASTES 9:9

When we talk about work and family and how to balance the two, the answer is not always less work. Sometimes it is integrating the family into your work. For example, does your job allow the opportunity for you and your spouse to have lunch together from time to time? Such lunches can be an oasis in the midst of a dry day.

If your job requires travel, could you take your spouse or one of your children with you? This allows a mini-vacation that you might not otherwise be able to afford. It also exposes your family to your vocation and gives them a little more appreciation for what you do.

Less work and more time at home is not necessarily the answer. Better use of time at home may make all the difference. Do something different tonight with a family member. Get out of the routine. Take initiative.

Such actions say, "I care about this relationship. I want to keep it alive. I enjoy being with you. Let's do something you would like to do." Minimize screen time; maximize activity and conversation. According to Ecclesiastes 9:9, the Bible says your spouse is a gift. Hard work is a necessary part of life, but a marriage partner is a reward and a blessing. When you remember that and prioritize accordingly, you will keep your marriage alive and growing.

Lord Jesus, I'm grateful for the gift of my spouse. Please help me to make him or her a priority. Show me creative ways to increase my time with him or her, and ways to make that time meaningful.

Helping Children Feel Loved

Always be humble and gentle. Be patient
with each other, making allowance for
each other's faults because of your love.
EPHESIANS 4:2

Do your children feel loved? I didn't ask, "Do you love
your children?" I know the answer to that. But if you
want to make sure your children *feel* loved, it is not
enough to be sincere. You also need to speak your child's
love language.

For some children, quality time is their primary
love language. If you don't give them quality time, they
will not feel loved, even if you are giving them words
of affirmation, physical touch, gifts, and acts of service. If your children are begging you to do things with
them, then quality time is likely their love language.
It's easy to get frustrated with the endless requests, but
we need to respond with gentleness and patience, as
Ephesians 4 reminds us. Bear with your kids, make

allowance for their faults, and look for the need behind their behavior. Give them some focused attention, and watch their behavior change.

Lord, you know how much I love my children. I want them to feel that love. Please give me the wisdom to communicate it the best way possible. Help me to have patience when they're asking for something and to see it as a signal for what they really need.

Admitting Negative Emotions

Laughter can conceal a heavy heart,
but when the laughter ends, the grief remains.
PROVERBS 14:13

Some Christians don't want to accept the fact that they have negative emotions. Anger, fear, disappointment, loneliness, frustration, depression, and sorrow don't fit the stereotype of successful Christian living. We often try to push negative emotions to the back burner and ignore them. That doesn't work very well, as King Solomon noted. We can ignore our negative feelings, but that doesn't make them go away. In fact, ignoring them can actually intensify them.

I believe that it is far more productive to identify and accept our emotions and then seek God's direction regarding what we are feeling. Feelings are like thermometers. They report whether we are hot or cold, whether all is well or not so well. If all is well, we can celebrate by praising God. (There are many biblical examples of this; see Psalm 103 for one.) If emotions indicate that all is not well, we can turn to God for help. (Again, see the Psalms for vivid examples of King David and others bringing strong feelings to God. Psalm 13 is one example.) God will give us wisdom if we need to take action. He can give us comfort if the situation cannot be changed. Always, we should share our emotions with God and seek his guidance.

"Lord, this is how I feel. Now, what do you want me to do about it?" This approach will lead to more insight about yourself, more empathy for your spouse, and more wisdom in your decisions. All this contributes to a growing marriage.

Lord, I am grateful for the Psalms, which show so clearly that you welcome us to express our emotions to you—whether positive or negative. Please help me to do that freely, rather than bottling up my sadness or anger. As you give me comfort and guidance, I know I will act more wisely, and that will benefit my relationship with my spouse.

Wise Listening

If you listen to constructive criticism, you will be
at home among the wise. If you reject discipline,
you only harm yourself; but if you listen to
correction, you grow in understanding.

PROVERBS 15:31-32

For thirty years, I've been counseling couples and leading marriage-enrichment seminars. I've never met a
couple who didn't have conflicts. I've met some who
knew how to resolve conflicts, and I've met many who
allowed conflicts to destroy their marriage.

One way to work through conflict is by setting
aside time each week for a "conflict resolution session."
When you sit down to discuss a conflict, take turns
talking. Start with five minutes each. You can have as
many turns as needed, but don't interrupt each other
with your own ideas. Wait for your turn. According to
King Solomon, listening to others—particularly if they
have constructive criticism to share with us—makes us
wise. When we listen to our spouse, especially during

conflict, we will gain more understanding of ourselves and each other.

You may ask questions to help you understand what your spouse is saying. For example, "Are you saying that you feel disappointed when I play golf on Saturday instead of spending time with you and the children? Are you saying that you would prefer that I not play golf at all?"

After listening, you then have your turn to talk. In this example, you might explain how important golf is to your mental health. Then together you can look for a solution that both of you agree is workable. Listening and seeking to understand each other is crucial in resolving conflicts.

Father, I want to be wise. Please help me to respond the right way when my spouse tells me something I don't necessarily want to hear. Help me to think about what is best for our relationship, not just about my own needs.

Conversational Prayer

Devote yourselves to prayer with
an alert mind and a thankful heart.
COLOSSIANS 4:2

The Bible makes clear that prayer is important. In Colossians 4, the apostle Paul encourages believers to "devote" themselves to prayer; in another epistle, he tells believers to "pray continually" (see 1 Thessalonians 5:17, NIV). We often take prayer for granted, but it's really an amazing concept. We can talk directly to the Creator of the universe! Why wouldn't we want to make that a habit with our spouse?

When counseling couples, I often talk about praying silently together with your spouse. It's the easiest way to get started. Today, I want to encourage you to try the next step: *conversational prayer*. In this approach, the two of you take turns talking to God. You may each pray one or more times about the same subject. Then one of you changes the subject, and you repeat the process. It's talking to God like you would talk to a friend.

For example, the husband might pray, "Father, God, thank you for protecting me on the way home from work today." The wife might then pray, "Yes, Father, I know that there are many accidents each day, and I sometimes take your protection for granted. I also want to thank you for protecting the children today." The husband prays, "I agree, and I pray especially that you will protect our kids from those who would pull them away from their faith." The wife prays, "Oh, Father, give us wisdom in how to teach our children to know and love you." And so, the conversation with God continues. It is an exciting way to pray with your spouse. Not only will it draw you closer to your heavenly Father, but it will draw you and your spouse closer together as you hear and pray about each other's concerns.

Father, God, I am amazed that I can talk to you at any time, and you hear me! What an incredible gift. Please help us to use this gift as a couple. I know that praying together will help us grow in our love for you and our love for each other. Give us the courage to get started and the discipline to continue.

Creating Spiritual Intimacy

Share each other's burdens, and in
this way obey the law of Christ.
GALATIANS 6:2

Most of the couples I meet wish that they could share more freely with each other about their spiritual journeys. We often speak of emotional intimacy or sexual intimacy, but we seldom talk about spiritual intimacy. Yet this affects all other areas of our relationship.

Just as emotional intimacy comes from sharing our feelings, spiritual intimacy comes from sharing our walk with God. We don't have to be spiritual giants to have spiritual intimacy as a couple, but we must be willing to share with each other where we are spiritually.

The husband who says, "I'm not feeling very close to God today" may not stimulate great joy in his wife's heart, but he does open the possibility for her to enter into his spiritual experience. If she responds with, "Tell me about it," she encourages spiritual intimacy.

If, however, she says, "Well, if you don't feel close to God, guess who moved?" she has stopped the flow, and he walks away feeling condemned. The apostle Paul challenged us to share each other's burdens, and those often include feelings of spiritual dryness or difficulty. Spiritual intimacy within a marriage requires a willingness to listen without preaching.

Father, I want to be able to talk with my spouse about my walk with you—and I want to hear about his or her experiences too. Please help us to be kind as we listen to each other and share each other's burdens. Develop spiritual intimacy in us, I pray.

Practical Tools for Making Time

> Be careful how you live. Don't live
> like fools, but like those who are wise.
> Make the most of every opportunity.
> EPHESIANS 5:15-16

I don't know anything that pays greater dividends than investing time in your marriage. It will affect your physical, mental, and spiritual health and the health of your spouse and children. It will also bring glory to the God who instituted marriage. A healthy marriage includes setting goals and making time for each other. I want to suggest two things that will help you meet those goals: delegating other responsibilities and scheduling time with your spouse.

When you consider delegating responsibilities, start with your children. How about making them responsible for washing dishes, clothes, and dogs? Or, if it's financially feasible, you can hire a neighborhood teen to mow your lawn or vacuum the carpet. Whatever you can pass off to others gives you more time to invest in your marriage. When your spouse says, "You know, I like the way we're becoming friends again," you'll know your investment is paying off.

The second suggestion is to reflect your priorities in your schedule. If your goal is to have dinner out at least once a week, do you have it on the calendar for this week? How about next week? If you don't schedule things, they are not likely to happen. I encourage you to sit down together with your calendars and write down all the times you plan to spend together, big and small. When you write your spouse into your schedule, you communicate that he or she is important to you. You are making the most of every opportunity, as the Scriptures suggest, and you're on the road to overcoming the barrier of time.

Father, thanks for these ideas that will help us meet the goals we've set for our relationship. Please help me to do my part to keep those goals at the forefront of my mind. My spouse is my highest priority after my relationship with you; please help me to remember that and act on it.

Seeking Reconciliation

Seek the LORD while you can find him. Call on him
now while he is near. Let the wicked change their ways
and banish the very thought of doing wrong. Let them
turn to the LORD that he may have mercy on them.
Yes, turn to our God, for he will forgive generously.

ISAIAH 55:6-7

Is the marriage over if your spouse walks out? The
answer is an emphatic *no*. Marital separation means
that the marriage needs help. The biblical ideal calls
for reconciliation. You may not feel like reconciling,
and you may see no hope for reunion. The process may
frighten you, but may I challenge you to follow the
example of God himself?

Throughout the Bible, God is pictured as having
a love relationship with his people—Israel in the Old
Testament and the church in the New Testament. On
many occasions, God found himself separated from
his people because of their sin and stubbornness. In a
sense, the entire Bible is a record of God's attempts to be
reconciled to his people. Note that God always pleaded
for reconciliation based on correcting sinful behavior.

Never did God agree to reconcile while Israel continued in sin. In the passage above, the prophet Isaiah passionately called people to turn away from their sins and toward the Lord. God was near, and his forgiveness was available.

There can be no reconciliation without repentance. In a marriage, that means mutual repentance, because the failure has involved both parties. Dealing with your own failures is the first step in seeking reconciliation.

Father, I am thankful for your example of calling for loving reconciliation. I confess my own sins in my marriage. Help me to deal with those first as I seek reconciliation with my spouse.

The Importance of Sex

Let me see your face; let me hear your voice. For
your voice is pleasant, and your face is lovely.
SONG OF SOLOMON 2:14

Why is sex such an important part of marriage? We
are sexual creatures by God's design. The most obvious
purpose of sexuality is reproduction, but that is not the
only one.

A second purpose is companionship. God said of
Adam, "It is not good for the man to be alone" (Genesis
2:18). God's answer was the creation of Eve and the
institution of marriage, about which Scripture says,
"The two are united into one" (Genesis 2:24). That's
true literally and metaphorically. In sexual intercourse,
we bond with each other. It is the opposite of being
alone. It is deep intimacy, deep companionship.

A third purpose of sex is pleasure. The Song of
Solomon is replete with illustrations of the pleasure
of relating to each other sexually within marriage. The

descriptive phrases may be foreign to our culture (an American man wouldn't typically compare his wife's teeth to sheep, for example), but the intent is clear: Maleness and femaleness are meant to be enjoyed by marriage partners.

Sex was not designed to be placed on the shelf after the first few years of marriage. God's desire is that we find and enjoy mutual sexual love throughout our married life.

Father, thank you for creating sex as a means for procreation, companionship, and pleasure. May all those purposes be fulfilled in our marriage.

Positive Influence

Imitate God, therefore, in everything you do,
because you are his dear children. Live a life filled
with love, following the example of Christ.
EPHESIANS 5:1-2

Have you ever heard, "You can't change someone else"? It's true that *you cannot change the person you love, but you can and do influence him or her every day.* That's the reality of marriage. If you are still trying to change your spouse, then you may be a manipulator. You reason, *If I do this, then my spouse will do that* or *If I can make him miserable enough or happy enough, then I'll get what I want.* I hate to discourage you, but you're on a dead-end road. Even if you manage to get your spouse to change, your manipulation will foster resentment.

A better approach is to be a positive influence on your spouse. You influence by your words and actions. If you look for something your spouse is doing that you like and give verbal compliments, you are having a positive influence. If you do something that you know your spouse will like, your actions have a wholesome influence. If you treat your spouse with respect and kindness, your example begins to rub off.

In Ephesians 5, Paul instructs us to follow the example of Christ and live with love. Just as a small boy imitates his father, so we should imitate our heavenly Father. When we follow that perfect model, we can't help but positively influence the ones we love. The reality of the power of positive influence holds tremendous potential for troubled marriages.

Lord, I know you are the perfect model of love, and I want to imitate you. As I do that, I pray that I would be a positive influence on my spouse.

Discovering Love Languages through Hurts

Search me, O God, and know my heart; try me and
know my anxious thoughts; and see if there be any
hurtful way in me, and lead me in the everlasting way.

PSALM 139:23-24 (NASB)

What does your spouse do or say that hurts you most
deeply? That is probably a clue to your primary love
language. The hurt may not come from what he does or
says, but rather what he fails to do or say. One wife said,
"He never lifts a hand to help me around the house. He
watches television while I do all the work. I don't understand how he could do that if he really loved me." Her
love language is *acts of service*. In her mind, if you love
someone, you do things to help. For her, actions speak
louder than words.

For others, words may speak louder than actions.
One husband told me, "All my wife ever does is criticize
me. I don't know why she married me. It's obvious she
doesn't love me." For him, if you love someone, you

speak kindly. His love language is *words of affirmation*, which is why her critical words hurt him so deeply.

If you want to discover your spouse's love language, you might ask, "What is it that I do or say, or fail to do or say, that hurts you most deeply?" It may be a scary question, but the answer will likely reveal his or her love language. Also, Psalm 139 tells us that if we ask God, he will reveal things in our lives that are hurtful to others. Ask him to give you insight as you broach the subject with your spouse.

Father, you know everything about me, including what I do that most hurts my spouse. Please reveal that to me. As I talk to my spouse, help me to have a heart that's willing to listen, learn, and improve so I can love my spouse more effectively.

Creating an
Atmosphere of Respect

In the same way, you husbands must give
honor to your wives. Treat your wife with
understanding as you live together.

1 PETER 3:7

When the word *intimacy* is mentioned, many husbands immediately think of sex. But sex cannot be separated from intellectual and emotional intimacy. The failure to recognize this reality leads to marital frustration.

If a woman does not feel free to express her ideas, or if she feels that her husband does not respect her ideas and will tell her they're foolish if she shares them, then she may have little interest in being sexually intimate with him. Her feelings of condemnation and rejection make it difficult for her to be sexually responsive.

If a wife does not feel loved by her husband, again the emotional distance stands as a barrier to sexual intimacy. A husband who ignores these realities will be frustrated at his wife's lack of interest in sex. The problem is not her lack of interest. Rather, it is the emotional barriers that exist between the two of them.

The apostle Peter encouraged men to honor their wives and treat them with understanding and consideration. Men should do this first and foremost because God commanded it, but the truth is that it benefits them as well. The wise husband will seek to create a climate where his wife feels accepted and loved as a person. In doing so, he opens the door to sexual intimacy.

Lord, I know that you always want us to treat each other with honor, respect, and love. When we do this, our relationship runs more smoothly— and it honors you. Help me to grow in this.

Finding Time
for the Oughts

Teach us to realize the brevity of life,
so that we may grow in wisdom.

PSALM 90:12

As Christians, we know that life's ultimate meaning is
to be found in relationships: first, in a relationship with
God, and second, in our relationships with people. On
the human level, the marriage relationship is designed
by God to be the most intimate, with the parent-child
relationship a close second. Yet some of us pursue activities that have little to do with building relationships.
How do we stop the merry-go-round and get off?

Have you heard people say, "I know that I ought
to, but I just don't have time"? Is it true that we don't
have time to do what we ought to do? The word *ought*
means to be bound by moral law, conscience, or a sense
of duty. If we are not accomplishing our *oughts*, then we
need to examine our use of time. Time is a resource the
Lord has given us, and like any other resource, we need

to be good stewards of it. Psalm 90:12, and many other verses in the Bible, underscores the bottom-line reason for using our time well—because our time on earth is limited. Time is a precious commodity we shouldn't waste.

Ultimately, we can control how we use our time. We can accomplish our goals for our closest relationships. Making time for what's important means that we must say no to things of lesser importance. Do you need to sit down and take a fresh look at how you are using your time? Then do it today.

Lord, you know best how quickly our days on earth pass by. I want to use my time in the best way possible, and that means investing it in my relationship with you and my relationship with my spouse. Help me to make wise decisions as I evaluate my priorities.

Returning to Emotional Love

Dear children, let's not merely say that we love each
other; let us show the truth by our actions.

1 JOHN 3:18

Falling in love is a temporary experience. It is not pre-
meditated; it simply happens in the normal context of
male-female relationships. What many people do not
know is that it is always temporary. The average life
span for being "in love" is two years.

The "in love" experience temporarily meets one's
emotional need for love. It gives us the feeling that
someone cares, that someone admires and appreciates
us. Our emotions soar with the thought that another
person sees us as number one. For a brief time, our
emotional need for love is met. However, when we
come down off the emotional high, we may feel empty.
That's sometimes accompanied by feelings of hurt, disappointment, or anger.

If emotional love is to return to your relationship,

it will require each of you to discover and speak each other's primary love language. As we've discussed, there are only five basic languages: words of affirmation, acts of service, gifts, quality time, and physical touch.

The apostle John recounted an important truth when he wrote his first epistle: Love can be expressed in words, but it is shown to be true through our actions. Learn the language of your spouse, speak it regularly, and emotional love will return to your marriage.

Lord God, I want us to feel strong, emotional love as a couple again. Please help us reach that point by committing to loving each other by our actions, not just our words. Help us to learn each other's love language and speak it well.

Confession and Forgiveness

Against you, and you alone, have I sinned; I have done
what is evil in your sight. You will be proved right
in what you say, and your judgment against me is
just. . . . Purify me from my sins, and I will be clean;
wash me, and I will be whiter than snow.

PSALM 51:4, 7

I wish that I were a perfect husband: always kind,
thoughtful, understanding, considerate, and loving.
Unfortunately, I am not. None of us are. I am sometimes selfish, thoughtless, and cold. In short, I fail to
live up to the biblical ideal for a Christian husband.
Does that mean that my marriage is destined for failure?
Not if I am willing to admit my failures and if my wife
is willing to forgive.

Forgiveness does not mean simply overlooking or
ignoring the other person's failures. God's forgiveness
should be our model. God forgives us based on what
Christ did for us on the cross. God does not overlook
sin, and God does not forgive everyone indiscriminately.
God forgives *when* we confess our sin and express our
need for forgiveness. Psalm 51, written by King David

after his sin with Bathsheba, is a helpful model of true remorse for wrongdoing. David admitted his guilt, acknowledged God's justice, and asked for God's purifying forgiveness. And God gave it to him.

Genuine confession always precedes true forgiveness. So, in order to have a growing marriage, I must confess my failures to my wife, and she must forgive me.

Father, it is often hard to confess my sins to my spouse. And it can be just as hard to forgive my spouse after I've been wronged. Please soften our hearts toward each other. Help us to forgive each other as you forgive us.

Love as the Cornerstone

We know how much God loves us, and we have put
our trust in his love. God is love, and all who live
in love live in God, and God lives in them.

1 JOHN 4:16

I really do believe that "love makes the world go 'round."
Why would I say that? Because God is love. It is his love
for us that makes all of life meaningful. First John 4
reminds us that when we realize how much God loves
us, it is so magnificent that we put our trust in that love.
Even those who do not believe in God are the recipients
of his love. He gives them life and the opportunity to
respond to his love. He wants to forgive and enrich their
lives. His plans for them are good.

What does all of this have to do with marriage? God
instituted marriage because he loved us. His intention
was certainly not to make us miserable; he made us
for each other. Husband and wife are designed to work
together as a mutually supportive team to discover and

fulfill God's plans for their lives. It's beautiful when it works.

What is the key to having that kind of marriage? In a word, *love*. It is the choice to look out for each other in the same way that God looks out for us. It is allowing God to express his love through us. It doesn't require warm feelings, but it does require an open heart.

Father, thank you for your amazing love for us. When we know you, we know the true definition of love, because you are love. I want to have this kind of love for my spouse, too. Please transform me and show me how to love my husband or wife this way.

Melding Words and Actions

Fathers, do not provoke your children to anger by the
way you treat them. Rather, bring them up with the
discipline and instruction that comes from the Lord.

EPHESIANS 6:4

If you have children, you know that the two wheels on
which the chariot of parenting rolls are *teaching* and
training. Teaching generally uses words to communicate with the child, and training uses actions. It is not
uncommon for one parent to emphasize words and
the other actions. One will want to talk the child into
obedience, while the other will simply make the child
obey. Both approaches have value, but when taken to an
extreme, each has its problems. One can lead to verbal
abuse and the other to physical abuse.

The Bible is clear that good parenting should not
"provoke . . . children to anger" or, as another translation states, "exasperate" them (NIV). While this verse
from Ephesians is directed to fathers, it certainly applies
to both parents, either of whom can anger a child by

unfair, disrespectful, or unnecessarily harsh treatment. The better approach is to bring words and actions together. Tell the child exactly what is expected and what the results of disobedience will be. Then if the child does not obey, kindly but firmly apply the consequences. When you are consistent, your child will learn obedience.

Rather than being competitors in parenting, why not team up and combine your skills to make helpful rules and determine consequences? The positive result is that both of you will know what to do if the child disobeys, and you'll be consistent. Of course, all of this works best when the child feels loved by both parents. Parenting is a team sport.

Lord, thank you for the chance to parent with my spouse as part of a team. Help us to work together to come up with the best approach for our children—one that doesn't exasperate them but helps mold them into the people you want them to be. Thank you for the family you have given us.

Encouraging Excellence

> Let us think of ways to motivate one another
> to acts of love and good works.
>
> HEBREWS 10:24

Marriage gives a husband and wife an opportunity to minister to each other. They accept each other as they are, but they can also encourage each other to excellence. God has plans for each life. Spouses can help each other succeed in accomplishing these plans, and often this is done by expressing love.

Not everyone feels significant. Some people grew up in homes where they were given negative messages: *You are not smart enough. You're not athletic or talented. You'll never amount to anything.* All these messages are false, but if they are all you have ever heard, you are likely to believe them.

When you learn your spouse's primary love language and speak it regularly, you are filling his love tank. You are also impacting her concept of herself. *If he loves me*, she thinks, *I must be significant.* You become God's agent for helping your spouse feel loved. Few things are more important in encouraging your spouse to accomplish God's plans. As the author of Hebrews wrote, as believers, we should consider how we can encourage each other to greater love and service. That's even more true within a marriage.

Marriage is designed to help us accomplish more for God. Two are better than one in his Kingdom.

Father, thank you for the plans you have for our lives. We are significant to you, and we can make a difference. Please help me to encourage my spouse in his or her walk with you.

Helping Your Loved One Succeed

Oh, the joys of those who . . . delight in the law
of the LORD, meditating on it day and night.
They are like trees planted along the riverbank,
bearing fruit each season. Their leaves never
wither, and they prosper in all they do.

PSALM 1:1-3

What is success? Ask a dozen people, and you may get a dozen different answers. A friend of mine said, "Success is making the most of who you are with what you've got." I like that definition. Every person has the potential to make a positive impact on the world.

Psalm 1 compares a successful person to a tree—planted by the riverbank, stable and with deep roots, healthy, flourishing, and fruitful. When we are deeply rooted in God, he can use us, and we can make a significant difference in the world. It all depends on what we do with what we have. Success is not measured by the amount of money we possess or the position we attain, but by how we use our resources and our opportunities. Position and money can be used to help others, or they can be squandered or abused. The truly successful people are those who help others succeed.

The same is true in marriage. A successful wife is one who expends her time and energy helping her husband reach his potential for God and for doing good in the world. Likewise, a successful husband is one who helps his wife do the same. If you help your spouse succeed, you end up living with a winner—and someone who feels fulfilled and purposeful. Not a bad life.

Heavenly Father, I want to be well-rooted in you and able to have a positive impact on those around me. I want that for my spouse, too. Please help me to make it my goal to help him or her succeed in making the most of his or her abilities.

Pursuing Reconciliation

If you are presenting a sacrifice at the altar in the
Temple and you suddenly remember that someone
has something against you, leave your sacrifice there
at the altar. Go and be reconciled to that person.
Then come and offer your sacrifice to God.

MATTHEW 5:23-24

In a perfect world, there would be no need for apologies. But in our imperfect world, we cannot survive without them. We are moral creatures; we have a strong sense of right and wrong. When we are wronged, we experience hurt and anger. The wrong becomes a barrier between the two people involved. In marriage, this creates tension, and our unity is threatened. Things are not the same in the relationship until someone apologizes and someone forgives.

When wrongdoing has fractured a relationship, something within us cries out for reconciliation. The desire for reconciliation is often more potent than the desire for justice. The more intimate the relationship, the deeper the desire for reconciliation. Reconciliation is so important to God that Jesus instructed his hearers to settle any offenses before offering a sacrifice to the Lord. Before we can humble ourselves before God, we need to humble ourselves and confess our wrong to those we have offended.

When a husband treats his wife unfairly, she often has two reactions. On the one hand, she wants him to pay for his wrongdoing; but at the same time, she wishes for reconciliation. It is his sincere apology that makes genuine reconciliation possible. If there is no apology, her sense of morality will push her to demand justice. Apologies are necessary for good relationships.

Father, I see how important reconciliation is to you. Thank you for reminding me that apologizing and forgiving are integral parts of a marriage. Help me to be willing to reconcile with my spouse so that our relationship will remain strong.

Affirming Words

Worry weighs a person down;
an encouraging word cheers a person up.

PROVERBS 12:25

Many couples have never learned the tremendous power of verbally affirming each other. Verbal compliments, or words of affirmation, are powerful communicators of love. King Solomon, author of the ancient Hebrew "wisdom literature" we find in the Bible, wrote several proverbs about words. The passage above, Proverbs 12:25, highlights the importance of encouraging words. Proverbs 18:21 is even more dramatic, saying, "The tongue can bring death or life." Cutting, critical comments can kill a person's spirit, but affirming words bring renewal and hope.

Read the following statements and ask yourself, *Have I said anything similar to my spouse within the last week?*

"You look sharp in that outfit."

"Wow! Do you ever look nice in that dress!"

"You have got to be the best potato cook in the world. I love these potatoes."

"Thanks for getting the babysitter lined up tonight. I want you to know I don't take that for granted."

"I really appreciate your washing the dishes."

"I'm proud of you for getting that positive job review. You're a hard worker, and it shows."

Want to improve your marriage? Say something positive to your spouse today.

Lord Jesus, why is it so much easier for me to criticize than to affirm? Please help me to train myself to notice the good things about my spouse—and to say something about them. I want my words to bring life, not discouragement. I need your help to develop new patterns, Lord.

Enhancing Communication

Don't use foul or abusive language. Let everything you
say be good and helpful, so that your words will be
an encouragement to those who hear them.

EPHESIANS 4:29

Learning to share your thoughts is the most foundational element of communication. In marriages that fail,
almost all couples say, "Our communication just broke
down." How do we keep this from happening? We do
what we did when we were courting: listen when the
other person talks. Listen without condemnation.

If your spouse comes up with a new idea that
surprises you, resist the urge to respond with criticism. Instead, ask questions. You might say, "That's an
interesting idea. If we tried to apply that to our marriage,
what would it look like? What need would this meet
for you? If we did it, what would be the downside?"
Questions like these can lead to meaningful dialogue.

Statements such as "That won't work for us" or
"I don't want to do that" stop conversation cold. It's

okay to have those thoughts and even okay to express them—if you do it in a positive way, *after* you have listened carefully to your spouse. You might say, "I'm afraid that might not work for us. I'm not sure that I really want to do it. Can we spend a few days thinking about it and then discuss it again?" That's being respectful and helpful, following the advice Paul gives in Ephesians 4. Our words to each other should be encouraging, not abusive or discouraging.

When you're keeping communication open and respectful, you're moving toward a growing marriage.

Father, when my spouse shares an idea with me, please give me the presence of mind to listen before I react. Let my words and questions be helpful and insightful as we come to agreement as a couple.

The Foundation of Spiritual Intimacy

No one can lay any foundation other than
the one we already have—Jesus Christ.

1 CORINTHIANS 3:11

Spiritual intimacy is often the most difficult area of marriage, and yet it is the most important. Our relationship with God affects everything else we do. The apostle Paul wrote in 1 Corinthians 3 that the only foundation for believers is Jesus Christ. Trusting in him for our salvation provides the basis and direction for the rest of our lives.

Obviously, we must each maintain our own personal walk with God. We cannot do that for each other. But as married partners, we can share that walk, and in so doing, we encourage each other and build intimacy. Let me share some ideas for improving spiritual intimacy:

1. Share with each other one thing you liked about the worship service you attended.

(That's far more edifying than sharing the things you did not like.)

2. Share a Scripture verse you read in your own devotional time. Don't use this to preach at your husband or wife, but to share what you found encouraging or insightful.

3. Pray together. Start with silent prayer if you like; hold hands and pray silently. Say amen aloud when you're finished and wait for your spouse to say amen. It is not that difficult, and it will draw you closer together.

Just as our relationship with God affects other aspects of our life, so spiritual intimacy will affect all other aspects of our marriage. As we each grow closer to God, we grow closer to each other. Spiritual intimacy will enhance emotional, intellectual, and physical intimacy. All of these are part of becoming *one* in marriage.

Lord Jesus, I know that you are the foundation of my life. Nothing else can take that most important place. I pray that our relationship with you would also be central to our marriage. Help us to share the challenges and encouragements we face as we grow nearer to you. May we draw closer together as our spiritual intimacy grows.

Our Need for Rest

On the seventh day God had finished his work
of creation, so he rested from all his work.

GENESIS 2:2

Physically, mentally, and emotionally, humans are designed with the need for rhythm between work and play. The old saying "All work and no play makes Jack a dull boy" reflects a fundamental human need for recreation or relaxation. This need is reflected in the second chapter of the Bible, where we learn that after Creation was completed, the Lord rested from his work. As people made in God's image, are we surprised that we also have this need?

Look at your own and your spouse's behavior, and you will see that at least some of your actions are motivated by this desire for recreation and relaxation. The methods of meeting this need are colored by our personality and preferences.

Why does Eric come home from work, click on the

TV, and enjoy his favorite drink before engaging in conversation with his wife? Because he wants to relax before he makes the effort to relate to her. Or why does Ashley stop at the gym before she comes home and interacts with her family? Consciously or unconsciously, she is seeking to meet her need for relaxation. If we understand our spouse's need, we can try to find a way to get the love we need and still allow our partner the freedom to meet his or her own needs. We, too, must find our own way of relaxing—whether it's reading, exercising, watching TV, or pursuing a hobby—or we will lose our emotional stability. The wise spouse encourages recreation and relaxation.

Father, thank you for the need to rest and relax. Too often, I view this as a waste of time, but I know it's an important need that you have given us. Help me not to criticize my spouse for relaxing, but to view it as a positive thing for refreshment.

Learning the Love Languages

Dear friends, since God loved us that much, we
surely ought to love each other. No one has ever
seen God. But if we love each other, God lives in us,
and his love is brought to full expression in us.

1 JOHN 4:11-12

My research indicates that there are five basic languages
of love:

- Words of affirmation—using positive words to
  affirm the one you love
- Gifts—giving thoughtful gifts to show you were
  thinking about someone
- Acts of service—doing something that you
  know the other person would like
- Quality time—giving your undivided attention
- Physical touch—holding hands, kissing,
  embracing, putting a hand on the shoulder, or
  any other affirming touch

Out of these five, each of us has a primary love language. One of these languages speaks more deeply to us than the others. Do you know your love language? Do you know your spouse's?

Many couples earnestly love each other but do not communicate their love in an effective way. If you don't speak your spouse's primary love language, he or she may not feel loved, even when you are showing love in other ways.

The Bible makes it clear that we need to love each other as God loves us. The apostle John wrote that God's love can find "full expression" in us. If that's true for the church in general, how much truer is it for a couple? Finding out how your loved one feels love is an important step to expressing love effectively.

———————————————

Father, help me to be a student of my spouse. I want to know how best to show my love. Please give me wisdom as I try to determine my beloved's love language.

Revealing Yourself in Marriage

The LORD gives righteousness and justice to all who
are treated unfairly. He revealed his character to
Moses and his deeds to the people of Israel.

PSALM 103:6-7

What do you know about the art of self-revelation? It all
began with God. God revealed himself to us through the
prophets, the Scriptures, and supremely through Christ.
As the verse above mentions, he revealed himself to the
ancient Israelites through his actions. They saw him
guiding them out of Egypt and into the Promised Land,
and as they did, they learned about him. If God had not
chosen self-revelation, we would not know him.

The same principle is true in marriage. Self-revelation
enables us to get to know each other's ideas, desires, frus-
trations, and joys. In a sense, it is the road to intimacy.
No self-revelation, no intimacy. So how do we learn the
art of self-revelation?

You can begin by learning to speak for yourself.
Communication experts often explain it as using "I"

statements rather than "you" statements. For example, "*I* feel disappointed that you are not going with me to my mother's birthday dinner" is very different from "*You* have disappointed me again by not going to my mother's birthday dinner." When you focus on your reaction, you reveal your own emotions. Focusing on the other person's actions places blame. "You" statements encourage arguments. "I" statements encourage communication.

Father, help me to remember that revealing more of myself is the first step toward greater intimacy with the one I love. Thank you for revealing yourself to us, and please give me the courage to share myself with my spouse.

How Do You Measure Your Life?

The generous will themselves be blessed,
for they share their food with the poor.

PROVERBS 22:9 (NIV)

Using credit to buy things is a huge issue in today's culture. The media screams, "Buy now, pay later." What is not stated is that if you "buy now," you will pay *much more* later. Interest rates on credit-card debt can be more than 21 percent.

Credit cards encourage impulse buying, and most of us have more impulses than we can afford to follow. This can lead to some extreme marital stress every month when the credit-card bill arrives. Rather than "buy now, pay later," why not agree as a couple that what you cannot afford, you will not purchase? Most of us can live with less, and perhaps live more happily. Jesus taught, "Life is not measured by how much you own" (Luke 12:15). Life finds its greatest meaning in relationships—first with God, then with our spouse, children, extended family, and friends. After a point, using our money for ourselves has little meaning or significance. But as Proverbs 22:9 points out, using our money generously for others—whether those we know or others who are in need—can bless us. It can strengthen our relationships, give us a sense of purpose, and encourage others.

Things have meaning only as they enhance relationships. Why must you have the biggest and best now, if doing so puts stress on your marriage? *Things* bring only momentary pleasure, while relationships last for a lifetime.

Father, it's easy to get caught up in things I think we need now. Please give me the right perspective. Help me to realize what is really meaningful—our relationship with you and others. May we invest heavily in those things.

Where Change Begins

Why worry about a speck in your friend's eye when
you have a log in your own? . . . First get rid of the
log in your own eye; then you will see well enough
to deal with the speck in your friend's eye.

MATTHEW 7:3, 5

Here's one conclusion I've drawn as a marriage coun-
selor: Everyone wishes his or her spouse would change.
"We could have a good marriage if he would just help
me more around the house." Or, "Our marriage would
be great if she was willing to have sex more than once
a month." He wants her to change, and she wants
him to change. The result? Both feel condemned and
resentful.

Jesus' words in Matthew 7 vividly illustrate the
problem. We think we see others' faults clearly, and we
put forth a lot of effort to try to correct them. But the
truth is, our own sin blinds us. If we haven't dealt with
our own failings, we have no business criticizing our
spouse's.

There is a better way: *Start with yourself*. Admit that

you're not perfect. Confess some of your most obvious failures to your spouse and acknowledge that you want to change. Ask for one suggestion each week on how you could be a better husband or wife. To the best of your ability, make changes. Chances are, your spouse will reciprocate.

Father, it's so much easier to concentrate on my spouse's flaws than to deal with my own. Please give me the courage to look at myself honestly. Help me today to try to change one thing that will make me a better marriage partner.

Sharing the Goal

At last the wall was completed to half
its height around the entire city, for the
people had worked with enthusiasm.

NEHEMIAH 4:6

As a couple, what is your shared goal? Perhaps it's a smoothly running home, a harmonious relationship, and a sense of fairness. Recently, a woman was in my office complaining that her husband didn't help her with household responsibilities. "We both work full-time," she said. "But he expects me to do everything around the house while he watches TV and unwinds. Well, maybe I need to unwind too." Clearly this couple had not defined their shared goal.

The players on an athletic team do not all perform the same tasks, but they do have the same goal. That was also true when Nehemiah led the Israelites to rebuild the wall around Jerusalem. Some of them rebuilt gates, some carried materials, and others stood guard, watching for those who wanted to sabotage the work. The individuals had separate tasks, but they were united in their ultimate goal: making the city of Jerusalem safe again.

If we want harmony and intimacy in our relationship, then we must each do our part of the work. A spouse who feels put upon is not likely to be interested in intimacy. Why not ask your spouse, "Do you feel that we make a good team around the house?" Let the answer guide your actions.

Father God, thank you for the great example of teamwork from the book of Nehemiah. I want to keep our end goal in mind as my spouse and I negotiate the tasks in our home. Help me to do my part willingly and lovingly.

Learning to Listen

Fools think their own way is right,
but the wise listen to others.
PROVERBS 12:15

We will never resolve conflicts if we don't learn to listen. Many people think they are listening when in fact they are simply taking a break from talking—pausing to reload their verbal guns. The above verse from Proverbs doesn't pull any punches when it calls those who don't listen *fools*. We may not like that word, but the truth is, refusing to listen reveals a lack of humility. Wise people listen to others—especially those they love. Genuine listening means seeking to understand what the other person is thinking and feeling. It involves putting ourselves in the other person's shoes and trying to look at the world through his or her eyes.

Here's a good sentence with which to begin: "I want to understand what you are saying because I know it is important." One man told me he made a sign that read, "I am a listener." When his wife started talking, he would hang it around his neck to remind himself of what he was doing. His wife would smile and say, "I hope it's true." He learned to be a good listener.

Lord Jesus, thank you for listening to me when I pray. Help me to listen to my spouse—really listen—so I can understand him or her better.

When It Doesn't Come Naturally

This is my commandment: Love each other in the
same way I have loved you. There is no greater love
than to lay down one's life for one's friends.

JOHN 15:12-13

I'm often asked, "What if your spouse's love language is
something that doesn't come naturally for you?" Maybe
his love language is *physical touch*, and you're just not
a toucher. Or *gifts*, but gifts are not important to you.
Perhaps her love language is *quality time*, but sitting
on the couch and talking for twenty minutes is your
worst nightmare. He wants *words of affirmation,* but
words don't come easily for you. Or she prefers *acts of
service*, but you don't find satisfaction in keeping the
house organized. So, what are you to do?

You learn to speak your partner's language. If it
doesn't come naturally for you, learning to speak it is an
even greater expression of love because it shows effort
and a willingness to learn. This speaks volumes to your
spouse. Also, keep in mind that your love language may

not come naturally for your loved one. Your spouse has to work just as hard to speak your language as you do to speak his or her language. That's what love is all about.

Jesus made it clear that we are to love each other as he loved us—and that is with the highest degree of sacrifice. Few of us are called to literally lay down our lives for others, but we are called to lay down our lives in small ways every day. Love is giving. Choosing to speak love in a language that is meaningful to your spouse is a great investment of your time and energy.

Lord Jesus, thank you for demonstrating for us the greatest kind of love. I'm in awe of your willingness to lay down your life for me. Thank you. Please help me to respond with a humble willingness to lay down my life for my spouse, even in smaller ways such as communicating in his or her love language.

Learning to Encourage

Let everything you say be good and
helpful, so that your words will be an
encouragement to those who hear them.
EPHESIANS 4:29

Not everyone is a born encourager, so I want to give
you some practical ideas on how to increase your word
power. First, *keep it simple.* Some people feel that they
must speak flowery words to be encouraging. I've sometimes called this Hallmark-itis. It's far better to use
simple, straightforward words that sound like you. Your
spouse will appreciate your genuine effort to express
encouragement.

Second, *mean what you say.* Affirming does not
mean lying or exaggerating to make your spouse feel
better about himself. If you're not being sincere, you'll
know it and your spouse will know it, so what's the
point? Better a small compliment that is sincere than a
long accolade that is all fluff.

Third, *keep the focus on your spouse, not on yourself.* If

your spouse tends to reflect a compliment back to you by saying, "Oh, you're far better than I in that area," gently turn the compliment back to her. The affirmation process is not about you but about the other person.

The Bible makes it clear that believers are to encourage one another. Ephesians 4:29 gives us a significant challenge—to let everything we say be good and helpful so that others may be encouraged. Doing so with your spouse will bring optimism and blessing to your marriage.

Lord God, as I seek to grow in encouraging my spouse, please help me to remember these three ideas. I want to make encouraging words a habit, because I know that is pleasing to you and that it will help our relationship as a couple to grow.

God's Power of Transformation

Jesus said, "Come to me, all of you who are weary
and carry heavy burdens, and I will give you rest.
Take my yoke upon you. Let me teach you, because
I am humble and gentle at heart, and you will find
rest for your souls. For my yoke is easy to bear,
and the burden I give you is light."

MATTHEW 11:28-30

Does God make a difference in marriage? Thousands of
couples will testify that he made a difference in theirs.
How does this transformation happen? First, we must
establish a relationship with God. This means that we
must come to him and acknowledge that we have walked
our own way and broken his laws. We tell him that we
need forgiveness and we want to turn from our sins.

He stands with open arms and says, "Come to me,
all of you who are weary and carry heavy burdens, and
I will give you rest." That's a beautiful and astounding
invitation. If we are willing to come to him, he will not
only forgive us but also send his Spirit to live inside us.

The Holy Spirit is the one who changes our attitudes.

When he is in control of our lives, we begin to look at things differently. He shows us that people are more important than things and that serving others is more important than being served. He works within us to produce wonderful character qualities such as love, patience, kindness, and gentleness (see Galatians 5:22-23). He alone can effect such substantial change in the way we think and act.

Do you see how these new attitudes would transform your relationship? Nothing holds greater potential for changing your marriage than asking God to come into your life, forgive your sins, and let you see the world the way he sees it.

Father God, thank you for inviting us to come to you.
I am so grateful for your forgiveness, your teaching,
and your Holy Spirit, who lives in me and directs me.
I need your transformation. Please help me
to allow you to change me.

Why Pray?

If my people who are called by my name will humble
themselves and pray and seek my face and turn from
their wicked ways, I will hear from heaven and will
forgive their sins and restore their land.

2 CHRONICLES 7:14

Bible professor Harold Lindsell once said, "Why
should we expect God to do *without* prayer what he has
promised to do *if* we pray?" The Bible contains many
calls to prayer, including God's words to Solomon,
as recorded in 2 Chronicles 7. *If* the people humbled
themselves and prayed after they sinned, God would
hear them, forgive them, and restore them. His invitation to us is clear: "Ask me and I will tell you remark-
able secrets you do not know about things to come"
(Jeremiah 33:3). The author of Hebrews tells us to
"come boldly" to God's throne, where we will receive
mercy and grace (4:16).

We come to God as our Father, knowing that
he wants to do good things for his children. But we
must be ready to receive them. Thus, he says, "keep on

asking, and you will receive what you ask for" (Matthew 7:7). Now, granted, God does not do everything that we request. He loves us too much and is too wise to do that. If what we request is not for our ultimate good, then he will do something better. His will is always right.

Couples who learn to pray together are simply responding to God's invitation. He wants to be involved in your marriage. Praying together is one way of acknowledging that you want his presence and his power. Through prayer, he can change your attitudes and your behavior. Remember, God is love, and he can teach you how to love each other. "Keep on asking."

Lord, I am amazed that you so often invite us to pray—to communicate with you, the Lord of the universe! I am grateful for the love and guidance you offer. Please help my spouse and me to take the time to pray together. May we "come boldly" to you and through our prayers be brought closer to each other and closer to you.

Loving through Words

Wise words satisfy like a good meal; the right words
bring satisfaction. The tongue can bring death or life.

PROVERBS 18:20-21

There are two basic ways to express love in a marriage: *words* and *deeds*. Today, we'll look at words. First
Corinthians 8:1 says, "Love edifies" (NKJV) or "builds
up" (NIV). So, if I want to love, I will use words that
build up my spouse. "You look nice in that outfit."
"Thanks for taking the garbage out." "I loved the meal.
Thanks for all your hard work." "I appreciate your
walking the dog for me Tuesday night. It was a real
help." All of these are expressions of love.

Proverbs 18:21 tells us, "Death and life are in the
power of the tongue" (NKJV). Words are powerful. You
can kill your spouse's spirit with negative words—words
that belittle, disrespect, or embarrass. You can give life
with positive words—words that encourage, affirm,
or strengthen. I met a woman some time ago who

complained that she couldn't think of anything good to say about her husband. I asked, "Does he ever take a shower?" "Yes," she replied. "Then I'd start there," I said. "There are men who don't."

I've never met a person about whom you couldn't find something good to say. And when you say it, something inside the person wants to be better. Say something kind and life giving to your spouse today and see what happens.

Lord Jesus, help me to remember that my words are powerful. I want to use them to build up and give life, not to cut down and bring discouragement. Please help me to use my words today to express love to my spouse.

Loving through Deeds

Dear children, let's not merely say that we love each
other; let us show the truth by our actions.

1 JOHN 3:18

In yesterday's reading, I suggested there are two basic
ways to express love to your spouse: through *words* and
through *deeds*. Today we'll look at deeds. As we see in
the verse above, the apostle John wrote that we should
show our love for each other through actions, not just
words. It can be easy to speak words, but our sincerity
is proved through what we do. *Do* something to show
your love.

Love is kind, the Bible says (see 1 Corinthians 13:4).
So, to express your love, find something kind and do it.
It might be giving him an unexpected gift or washing
the car that he drives. It might be offering to stay home
with the children while she goes shopping or hiking. Or
perhaps it's picking up dinner on the way home when

you know she's had a hectic day. How long has it been since you wrote your spouse a love letter?

Love is patient (see 1 Corinthians 13:4). So, stop pacing the floor while your spouse is getting ready to go. Sit down, relax, read your Bible, and pray. Love is also courteous. Another way to say it might by *courtly*. So, do some of the things you did when you were courting. Reach over and touch his knee or take her hand. Open the door for her. Say please and thank you. Be polite. Express your love by your actions.

Lord, I know that both words and actions are important. Please help me to express my love through the things I say and do. I want to show my spouse how sincere my love is.

Listen First, Then Respond

If only someone would listen to me!
Look, I will sign my name to my defense.

JOB 31:35

Most of us share our ideas much too soon. We talk before we have really listened. In fact, one research project found that the average person will listen only seventeen seconds before interrupting.

The book of Job gives many illustrations of poor listening. As Job suffered with physical illness, grief, and loss of material things, he steadfastly maintained his good standing before God. But his "friends" brushed him off and stated insistently that he must have committed some great sin for God to allow him to suffer so much. Finally, after pages of speeches, Job gets fed up. We can hear his frustration in his words: "If only someone would listen to me!"

A good listener will never share his ideas until he is sure that he understands what the other person is saying. In marriage, this is extremely important. Ask questions, repeat what you think your spouse is saying, and ask, "Am I understanding you?" When your spouse says, "Yes, I think you understand what I'm saying and how I feel," then and only then are you ready to move on. You might say, "I really appreciate your being open with me. Now that I understand where you're coming from, may I share what I was thinking when I did that? I realize now that what I said was hurtful, but I want you to understand that I was not trying to hurt you." At this point, your spouse will hear your perspective, because you have first taken the time to really hear what he or she was saying.

Lord, I want to be a good and thoughtful listener. Let me not frustrate my spouse by expressing my opinions too soon and too strongly. Please give me ears to listen well.

Finding a Solution

I praise you because I am fearfully and wonderfully
made; your works are wonderful, I know that full well.

PSALM 139:14 (NIV)

Because we are all human, we all have conflicts as
couples. We all see the world differently. The common
mistake is to try to force our spouse to see the world
the way we see it. "If she would just think, I know she
would agree with me. My way makes sense." The problem is that what makes sense to one person does not
always make sense to another. Precision is fine in math
and science, but it does not exist in human relationships. As Psalm 139 makes clear, the Lord has made
each one of us unique. He formed us and knew us even
before we were born. We need to celebrate those differences, not let them frustrate us. We must allow for
differences in human perceptions and desires.

Resolving conflicts requires that we treat our spouse's
ideas and feelings with respect, not condemnation. The

purpose is not to prove our spouse wrong but to find a "meeting of the minds"—a place where the two of us can work together as a team. We don't have to agree in order to resolve a conflict. We simply have to find a workable solution to our differences.

"What would be workable for you?" is a good place to begin. Now we are focusing on resolution rather than differences. Two adults looking for a solution are likely to find one.

Father, this question—What would be workable for you?—is eye opening. How often I waste time trying to convince my spouse that my way is right. Please help me instead to join with him or her in looking for a solution that works for both of us. Thank you for making us both unique.

Finding Compromise

Wise words bring many benefits, and hard work
brings rewards. Fools think their own way
is right, but the wise listen to others.

PROVERBS 12:14-15

In making decisions, husbands and wives often disagree. If we don't learn how to come together, we may
spend a lifetime fighting. In yesterday's devotion, I said
that agreement requires listening, understanding, and
compromise. Compromise expresses a willingness to
move. It is the opposite of being rigid. King Solomon
said it bluntly in Proverbs 12: "Fools think their own
way is right, but the wise listen to others." If we respect
our spouse as our partner, we should also respect his or
her viewpoint. It's neither wise nor loving to cling to
our own viewpoint to the exclusion of our mate.

There are three possible ways to resolve a disagreement. One is what I call "Meet you on your side."
In other words, you might say, "Now that I see how
important this is to you, I'm willing to do what you

want." You agree to do it your spouse's way for his or her benefit.

A second possibility is "Meet you in the middle." This means you might say, "I'd be willing to give a little if you could give a little, and we'll meet in the middle." For example, "I'll go with you to your mother's for the Friday night dinner if you will return with me Saturday morning in time for the big game."

The third possibility is "Meet you later." A couple in this position might say, "We don't seem to be making any progress. Why don't we just agree to disagree and discuss it again next week?" In the meantime, call a truce and treat each other kindly.

Father, thank you for these ideas on how to compromise. Please help me to let go of my need to do things my way. You know that I love my spouse and want to respect his or her ideas. I want to commit to loving compromise as we make decisions.

Working as a Team

Two people are better off than one, for they
can help each other succeed. If one person
falls, the other can reach out and help. But
someone who falls alone is in real trouble.

ECCLESIASTES 4:9-10

Many couples enter marriage with the assumption that
their household will be run the way their parents did it.
The problem is, there are two moms and dads, and they
probably didn't do things the same way. Your parents and
your spouse's parents didn't have the same game plan;
so, as husband and wife, you naturally have very different expectations. What's the answer? You must construct
your own game plan along with your spouse.

Make a list of all the household responsibilities that
come to your mind. Washing dishes, cooking meals,
buying groceries, vacuuming the carpet, washing the
car, mowing the grass, paying the bills—everything. Ask
your spouse to do the same. Then put your two lists
together and come up with a "master list" of responsibilities. Next, each of you should take the list and put

your initials by the things you think should be your responsibilities. Finally, get together and see where you agree. The differences will need to be negotiated, with someone being willing to take responsibility.

Try it for six months and then evaluate how things are going. Do you feel the responsibilities are divided fairly? Is one person struggling with a certain task that perhaps the other could do more easily? What changes need to be made?

As you talk through these issues, remember that you're on the same team. As Ecclesiastes 4 says, two people working together can help each other succeed. Isn't that what you want for your marriage? Use your strengths to help each other.

Lord God, I am grateful for my spouse and for the chance to work as a team to keep our household and family running smoothly. I want to help my spouse succeed, Lord. Please guide us as we come up with a plan for handling responsibilities. Help me to communicate in love.

Our Primary Need

Three things will last forever—faith, hope, and love—
and the greatest of these is love.

1 CORINTHIANS 13:13

Love and marriage—they go together like a horse and carriage. Right? Well, they should, and in a healthy marriage, they do. Most people agree that our deepest emotional need is to feel loved. The apostle Paul even identifies love as the greatest thing, and King David wrote that God's "unfailing love is better than life itself" (Psalm 63:3). There's no question that God's steady love for us can be our emotional rock. But we also need to experience human love. And if we are married, the person whose love we long for the most is our spouse. In fact, if we feel loved, everything else is workable. If we don't feel loved, our conflicts become battlefields.

Now, don't misunderstand me. I'm not suggesting that love is our only need. Psychologists have observed that we also have basic emotional needs for security, self-worth, and significance. However, love interfaces with all of these.

If I feel loved, then I can relax, knowing that my spouse will do me no ill. I feel secure in his or her presence. I can face the uncertainties in my vocation. I may have enemies in other areas of my life, but with my spouse I feel secure.

Lord Jesus, thank you for your love that never fails. And thank you for the love I can share with my spouse. Please help me to love effectively, so that he or she will feel secure in our relationship.

Love Does Not Seek Its Own

[Paul said,] "I have been a constant example of
how you can help those in need by working hard.
You should remember the words of the Lord Jesus:
'It is more blessed to give than to receive.'"

ACTS 20:35

Happiness is a unique commodity. It is never found by the person shopping for it. Lonely men and women in every age have admitted the futility of their search for happiness, most notably King Solomon in the book of Ecclesiastes. This wealthy, powerful king, with servants to cater to his every whim, found most things in life to be tedious, meaningless, and devoid of joy.

Most of us get married assuming that we are going to be happy. After the wedding, we find that our mate does not always seek to make us happy. Perhaps our spouse even demands more and more of our time, energy, and resources for his or her own happiness. We feel cheated and used, so we fight for our rights. We demand that our spouse do certain things for us, or we give up and seek happiness elsewhere.

Part of the apostle Paul's definition of love in 1 Corinthians 13 is that it is "not self-seeking." Genuine happiness is the by-product of making someone else happy. I wonder what would have happened if King Solomon had found someone to serve? Doesn't Acts 20:35 say, "It is more blessed to give than to receive"?

Do you want to be happy? Discover someone else's needs and seek to meet them. Why not begin with your spouse? "How may I help you?" is a good question with which to begin.

Lord Jesus, you told us that blessing comes from giv-
ing, not receiving. Please help me to turn around
my expectations. I don't want to waste my time and
energy grasping at happiness only to be disappointed.
Instead, show me how to reach out to my spouse, giv-
ing to him or her. I want to bring happiness to my
mate through the way I express my love.

What Is Your Legacy?

Follow my example, as I follow the example of Christ.
1 CORINTHIANS 11:1 (NIV)

Among the things you will leave behind when you die is a marital legacy. Your example will without a doubt influence the lives of your children and others who observe it. Few things are more important than building the kind of marriage that you would be happy to have your children emulate.

When I ask older parents, "What do you wish for your adult children?" their response is often, "I want them to be happily married and to rear their children to be loving, caring citizens." That's a worthy goal. What are you doing to foster that goal? I want to suggest that the model of your own marriage is the greatest factor in helping your children have happy marriages.

The question is, will you leave a positive or a negative legacy? Many young adults struggle greatly because of the influence of the negative example set by their parents' marriage. Others are blessed greatly by a positive model.

It is not too late. As long as you are alive, you have time to work on the marital legacy you will leave behind. The best thing we can do is what Paul did: follow the example of Christ. The more closely we follow Jesus and treat each other the way he calls us to, the more Christlike our legacy will be.

Lord Jesus, I know that the only way I can leave a strong legacy is by following your example. Please help me to become more and more like you in the way I treat my spouse and the way I approach our marriage. I want to leave a positive example for those around us. Thank you, Lord.

Love Note
STARTER KIT

No matter what your primary love language is, it's always a good idea to learn how to put into words what you appreciate most about your spouse and to express your desire to "speak" his or her love language. On the following pages you will find a few simple prompts to help you compose a love note to your spouse that will directly address your respective love languages.

ACTS OF SERVICE

Serve one another in love.
GALATIANS 5:13

1. If *your* love language is acts of service, write a love note to your spouse describing what you appreciate about his or her efforts to "speak" your love language. Not every act of service has to be a grand gesture, so give your spouse a few suggestions of some simple things that he or she can do that you would find meaningful.

2. If your *spouse's* love language is acts of service, write a love note expressing your desire to learn how to "speak" his or her love language. Ask for suggestions of some simple things that you can do that he or she would find meaningful— perhaps something your spouse would enjoy that you might not know.

3. Set aside time this week to talk with your spouse about how you can learn to "speak" each other's primary love language.

WORDS OF AFFIRMATION

*How sweet your words taste to me;
they are sweeter than honey.*

PSALM 119:103

1. If *your* love language is words of affirmation, write a love note to your spouse describing what you appreciate about his or her efforts to "speak" your love language. Not all words of affirmation carry the same weight, so give your spouse a few suggestions of some simple things that he or she can say that you would find meaningful.

2. If your *spouse's* love language is words of affirmation, write a love note expressing your desire to learn how to "speak" his or her love language. Ask for suggestions about aspects of his or her life where your words would be most affirming— maybe it has to do with work, the home, your family, or some activity he or she particularly enjoys.

3. Set aside time this week to talk with your spouse about how you can learn to "speak" each other's primary love language.

RECEIVING GIFTS

Everyone is the friend of a person who gives gifts!
PROVERBS 19:6

1. If *your* love language is receiving gifts, write a love note to your spouse describing what you appreciate about his or her efforts to "speak" your love language. Not every gift has to be a grand gesture, so give your spouse a few suggestions of some simple gifts that he or she can give that you would find meaningful.

2. If your *spouse's* love language is receiving gifts, write a love note expressing your desire to learn how to "speak" his or her love language. Ask for suggestions of some simple gifts you can give that he or she would find meaningful—perhaps something your spouse would enjoy that you might not know.

3. Set aside time this week to talk with your spouse about how you can learn to "speak" each other's primary love language.

QUALITY TIME

You will show me the way of life,
granting me the joy of your presence.
PSALM 16:11

1. If *your* love language is quality time, write a love note to your spouse describing what you appreciate about his or her efforts to "speak" your love language. Not all time together carries the same weight, so give your spouse a few suggestions of some simple things you can do together that you would find meaningful.

2. If your *spouse's* love language is quality time, write a love note expressing your desire to learn how to "speak" his or her love language. Not all time together carries the same weight, so ask your spouse for suggestions about some simple things you can do together that he or she would find meaningful—perhaps something your spouse would enjoy that you might not know.

3. Set aside time this week to talk with your spouse about how you can learn to "speak" each other's primary love language.

PHYSICAL TOUCH

He took them in his arms and blessed them,
laying his hands on them.
MARK 10:16 (ESV)

1. If *your* love language is physical touch, write a love note to your spouse describing what you appreciate about his or her efforts to "speak" your love language. There is a lot more to the love language of physical touch than just sex, so give your spouse a few suggestions of some nonsexual touch that you would find meaningful.

2. If your *spouse's* love language is physical touch, write a love note expressing your desire to learn how to "speak" his or her love language. Hugs, pats on the back, holding hands, and thoughtful touches on the arm, shoulder, or face can all be ways to show concern, care, and love. Ask your spouse for suggestions of how to give physical touch in ways that he or she will find meaningful.

3. Set aside time this week to talk with your spouse about how you can learn to "speak" each other's primary love language.

About the Author

DR. GARY CHAPMAN is the author of the perennial bestseller *The Five Love Languages* (over four million copies sold) and numerous other marriage and family books. He also coauthored a fiction series based on *The Four Seasons of Marriage* with bestselling author Catherine Palmer. Dr. Chapman is the director of Marriage and Family Life Consultants, Inc.; an internationally known speaker; and the host of *A Love Language Minute*, a syndicated radio program heard on more than two hundred stations across North America. He and his wife, Karolyn, live in North Carolina.

ALSO AVAILABLE
— FROM —
GARY CHAPMAN

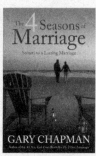

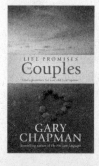